A Glimpse of Heaven

THROUGH THE EYES OF

C. S. LEWIS, DR. TONY EVANS,
CALVIN MILLER, RANDY ALCORN, J. OSWALD SANDERS,
JOHN WESLEY, AND OTHERS

Compiled by
Richard Leonard and JoNancy Linn Sundberg

New York London Toronto Sydney

Our purpose at Howard Books is to:
• *Increase faith* in the hearts of growing Christians
• *Inspire holiness* in the lives of believers
• *Instill hope* in the hearts of struggling people everywhere
Because He's coming again!

HOWARD BOOKS

Howard Books, a division of Simon & Schuster, Inc.
1230 Avenue of the Americas, New York, NY 10020
www.howardpublishing.com

A Glimpse of Heaven © 2007 by Howard Books

All rights reserved, including the right to reproduce this book or portions thereof in any form whatsoever. For information address Howard Subsidiary Rights Department, 1230 Avenue of the Americas, New York, NY 10020.

First Howard trade paperback edition October 2007

HOWARD and colophon are registered trademarks of Simon & Schuster, Inc.

For information regarding special discounts for bulk purchases, please contact Simon & Schuster Special Sales at 1-800-456-6798 or business@simonandschuster.com.

Compiled by Richard Leonard and JoNancy Linn Sundberg

Produced with the assistance of the Livingstone Corporation (www.LivingstoneCorp.com). Project staff includes Pete Gregory, Joan Guest, Mary Larsen, Joan Woodhead, and Sharon Wright.

Cover design by David Carlson
Interior design by Davina Mock-Maniscalco

Manufactured in the United States of America

10 9 8 7 6 5 4 3 2 1

Unless otherwise noted, Scripture quotations are taken from the *Holy Bible, New International Version*; copyright © 1973, 1978, 1984 by International Bible Society; used by permission of Zondervan; all rights reserved. Scripture quotations marked GNB are taken from the *Good News Bible in Today's English Version, Second Edition*; copyright © 1992 by American Bible Society; used by permission. Scripture quotations marked KJV are taken from the *Holy Bible, King James Version.* Scripture quotations marked NASB are taken from the *New American Standard Bible*®; copyright © The Lockman Foundation 1960, 1962, 1963, 1968, 1971, 1973, 1975, 1977; used by permission (www.Lockman.org). Scripture quotations marked NKJV are taken from the *New King James Version*®; copyright © 1982 by Thomas Nelson Inc.; used by permission; all rights reserved. Scripture quotations marked PHILLIPS are taken from *The New Testament in Modern English, Revised Edition* by J. B. Phillips; copyright © 1958, 1960, 1972 by J. B. Phillips.

Library of Congress Cataloging-in-Publication Data is available

ISBN-13: 978-1-4165-4392-3
ISBN-10: 1-4165-4392-9

In memory of loved ones who have seen heaven for themselves
and have no need of this book

Robert G. Sundberg (1931–1993)
Janice Akens Leonard (1937–1998)
Barbara R. Forte Leonard (1938–2001)
Clyde L. Malmgren (1936–1991)
Alton Hardy Howard (1925–2006)
Jason Blue Boultinghouse (1979–2006)

*We know that if our earthly house of this tabernacle were dissolved,
we have a building of God, an house not made with hands, eternal in the heavens.*
(2 *Corinthians* 5:1 KJV)

Contents

Chapter 3: Longing for Heaven

Chapter 4: At Home in Heaven

Chapter 5: Our Glory in Heaven

Chapter 6: Loved Ones in Heaven

Chapter 7: Hosts of Heaven

Chapter 8: Treasure in Heaven

Chapter 9: The Heavenly City

Chapter 10: Worship in Heaven

Chapter 11: Not in Heaven

Chapter 12: Influence of Heaven

Acknowledgments

With deep gratitude we acknowledge the encouragement and valued assistance of Shirley Anne Leonard, Richard Leonard's patient wife and research assistant; Inge Schilder, JoNancy Sundberg's resource-full and proofreading friend; Joan Guest, our astute project manager at The Livingstone Corporation; Keith Call, Wheaton College Special Collections, who provided some excellent sources.

We always thank God for all of you. . . . We continually remember before our God and Father your work produced by faith, your labor prompted by love, and your endurance inspired by hope in our Lord Jesus Christ.

(*1 Thessalonians 1:2–3*)

Preface

How great shall be that felicity, which shall be tainted with no evil, which shall lack no good, and which shall afford leisure for the praises of God, who shall be all in all!

—Aurelius Augustine, *The City of God*

Scripture repeatedly makes clear that heaven is a realm of unsurpassed joy, unfading glory, undiminished bliss, unlimited delights, and unending pleasures.

—John F. MacArthur, *The Glory of Heaven*

What a pleasure is there in the heavenly kingdom, without fear of death; and how lofty and perpetual a happiness with eternity of living!

—Cyprian, *Treatise VII: On the Morality*

Since heaven itself is God's temple, every place we go, everything we do, and every conversation we have will be an act of worship.

—Dr. Tony Evans, *The Best Is Yet to Come*

"Gracious Father, we have assembled ourselves at a point in time when time and eternity come so close that we can almost see the sparks."

As the pastor prayed at the memorial service, I asked myself, *Is my life so comfortable, my table so bountiful, the world God gave us so beautiful, the education so attainable, the godly examples so available, that there is no longing for anything better?* Have I lost sight of those sparks that ignite at the time of a homegoing, when "time and eternity come so close?" Or am I, with Abraham, "looking forward to the city with foundations, whose architect and builder is God" (Hebrews 11:10)?

Heaven is magnificent beyond our comprehension and more satisfying than anything we have ever known. And it has been prepared for those of us who believe our risen Lord has provided the way for us to live eternally with Him.

Why read a book like this on the subject of heaven?

I am so glad you asked!

1. *Eternity is a very long time!* Our lives here are but a speck of dust on the continuum of eternity. This earthly life, which we know so well, is infinitesimal compared to the endless ages of the past and those to come. Would you not like to know more about your REAL home?
2. *There is great joy in learning now about the God with whom we will spend eternity.* By reading about heaven, we discover more about who He is and what He does. We see His creativity, majesty, glory, and sovereign power. We enjoy the anticipation of living in His presence forever.
3. *We find purpose in this life by living in the light of eternity.* A heavenly perspective changes the way we invest the resources given to us—our time, our energy, our money, and everything else God has given us. We consider the importance of souls rather than the things of this earthly realm. We become virtually blinded to temporal concerns in the bright light of eternity. Holy living becomes a priority. We are preparing to meet the King!
4. *Our broken hearts and shattered dreams are healed by heaven.* The sufferings and tragedies of this life are placed in proper perspective when we set our hearts on heaven. We have comfort that the trials of *this* world are preparing us for an "eternal weight of glory" (2 Corinthians 4:17 KJV) in the next. We have hope of being reunited *for eternity* with loved ones. Better yet, we have assurance of meeting our most glorious God and Father, spending eternity basking in the glory of His presence. Thus, the ultimate tragedy of life—death—becomes the means by which we are given the greatest gift known: eternal life with God.

5. *We are motivated to spread the Good News so that others might someday join in the triumphal celebration.* We are the bearers of the *only* message that offers salvation from sin and death and a promise of eternal life. What a tremendous responsibility. What an awesome privilege.

We pray that as a result of reading this book, you will have increased passion for God's eternal glory. It's our hope that time and eternity will come so close that you will almost see the sparks!

—JoNancy Linn Sundberg

Introduction

In my Father's house are many mansions: if it were not so, I would have told you. I go to prepare a place for you. (John 14:2 KJV)

SUCH ARE THE WORDS OF CHRIST HIMSELF, who made clear the span of our years on this globe is not the sum total of our stories. We have each been "fearfully and wonderfully made" (Psalm 139:14). Perhaps life has been rich with purpose, accomplishment, knowledge, service, and passion—or perhaps not quite so rich, but still worth clinging to, we think! Whatever the circumstance, *life itself* is a precious and mysterious gift we do not understand. For those who believe firmly that it is "God, who gives life to everything" (1 Timothy 6:13), it is impossible to believe that He would, in the end, simply "leave us in the dust," as Tennyson said. For it is God who has "set eternity in the hearts of men" (Ecclesiastes 3:11).

We who look to the risen Lord as our hope must believe there is more to life than our allotted "seventy years—or eighty, if we have the strength" (Psalm 90:10) on this earthly plane that only grudgingly yields us its fruits and satisfactions. We look beyond, trusting Scripture's promise that "he who raised Christ from the dead will also give life to your mortal bodies through his Spirit, who lives in you" (Romans 8:11).

But what, indeed, lies *beyond?* What is to become of us when our days here reach their end, when "the spirit returns to God who gave it" (Ecclesiastes 12:7), and our flesh molders in the ground or our ashes scatter to the winds? Christians, and even many who did not yet know the name of Christ, have long wondered about these things. For those who seek its refuge, the life that lies ahead goes by many names: heaven, paradise, eternity, the afterlife, the resurrection. Through the ages Christians have wondered about it, inquired into it, meditated on it, preached it, and written about it in tractate and treatise, sermon and song, hymn and poem.

For Christians, the Holy Scriptures have been the only open window into the world beyond. In telling us of that world, the Scriptures "speak of God's secret wisdom" (1 Corinthians 2:7). The Bible gives us little information about heaven, in and of itself. It does not answer the question, What will things be like after we die? Rather, it answers, How should we then live? (see 2 Corinthians 5:14–18).

Some things we know. Heaven is where "the God of heaven" rules. It is where His will is done, as we pray it will be done on earth! Heaven is where the ascended Christ rules at His Father's right hand. In heaven, a host of messengers, or angels, serve God and rejoice when one of His earthly children turns away from sin (see Luke 15:7). In special instances heaven opens, and a seer catches a momentary glimpse of God's glory and truth (see Ezekiel 1:1, Revelation 19:11). Out of heaven comes the "holy city," the community in which God dwells in renewed covenant with His people (Revelation 21:2–3). So perhaps we know a few other things about heaven from the Word of God. But such hard data is sparse, and the search for it is complicated by the fact that the biblical words for heaven also refer to the sky—the earth's own starry, sunny, or cloudy firmament.

We are left to wonder, then, about many things concerning heaven. Indeed, it would seem that the Lord would have it so. For the apostle Paul himself, caught up to the "third heaven" in an experience we can only wonder about today, "heard inexpressible things, things that man is not permitted to tell" (2 Corinthians 12:4). There is a knowledge that is appropriate for the hosts of heaven, and another kind of knowledge appropriate for earth dwellers—namely, those things of the gospel that "even angels long to look into" (1 Peter 1:12).

So Christians, desiring to inquire into the mysteries of heaven while remaining faithful to the Word of God, are left with its *hints of heaven*—things not directly stated, but inferred from symbol, suggestion, story, or song. What kind of place has God prepared for those He loves, and who love Him? As noted preacher Lyman Abbott wrote a century ago, "I would not lay too much stress on the intimations of Scripture. I recognize the difference between its clear revelation and its poetic suggestions; but so far as its suggestions may be counted of value, they all indicate the continuance there of love, which alone makes life worth living here" (*The Other Room,* 1903). What he seems to be saying is that, while many inferences about heaven from Scripture are just that—clues or implications upon which no test of doctrine can be mounted—these inferences are still of great value for the comfort and edification of the people of God. The Bible's hints of heaven inspire us to pursue not only glory "then and there" but also godliness "here and now."

Those who have probed the subject of heaven, then, are offering us not certain knowledge so much as hope and aspiration, in much the same way that prophets in the church offer their insights. The end of all of this is not that we might be better informed, but for our "strengthening, encouragement and comfort" (1 Corinthians 14:3). In exploring heaven, the authors whose works are brought together in this volume have approached it from a variety of perspectives. Some have written with longing, even wistfulness. Some have brought humor or fancy into their work. Some have applied a dispassionate scholarship and a wide-ranging grasp of the Scriptural witness, while others have written more out of their intense and very personal love for the Lord. The literature included in this book spans the spectrum from the sentimental and devotional, through the artistic and esoteric, to the intellectual—and even, perhaps, the pedantic.

"Who has known the mind of the Lord?" asks the apostle Paul, "Or who has been his counselor?" (Romans 11:34). We understand that God's thoughts are not ours (see Isaiah 55:8). When we ponder what has not been completely revealed to us, we are forced to speak of it in language drawn from what *has* been made known. We project the roads past the edge of the map, trusting that they will intersect at a point of truth. Thus, some Christians through the centuries have painted their portraits of heaven using images drawn from the sinless paradise of Eden. Others have drawn from the bold imagery of the "new Jerusalem" come to earth. Still others have mingled the two or have perhaps added details from the riches of Christian experience that seem to demand a further development not attained during our earthly walk with the Lord.

We, the compilers and the publishers, hope and pray that the testimony of these authors will bring both illumination and consolation to readers of this volume and will strengthen them, one and all, in "hope that is stored up for [us] in heaven" (Colossians 1:5).

—Richard Leonard

CHAPTER 1

The Call of Heaven

Persuaded of a Future Life

ATHENAGORAS—SECOND CENTURY

FOR IF WE BELIEVED that we should live only the present life, then we might be suspected of sinning, through being enslaved to flesh and blood, or overmastered by gain or carnal desire; but since we know that God is witness to what we think and what we say both by night and by day, and that He, being Himself light, sees all things in our heart, we are persuaded that when we are removed from the present life we shall live another life, better than the present one, and heavenly, not earthly (since we shall abide near God, and with God, free from all change or suffering in the soul, not as flesh, even though we shall have flesh, but as heavenly spirit), or, falling with the rest, a worse one and in fire; for God has not made us as sheep or beasts of burden, a mere by-work, and that we should perish and be annihilated. On these grounds it is not likely that we should wish to do evil, or deliver ourselves over to the great Judge to be punished.

ATHENAGORAS was an Athenian philosopher active in the latter part of the second century. It is said that he wrote against Christianity, but after his conversion he became an apologist for the faith. As a writer, he had a clear style and was forceful in his arguments, and was the first to elaborate a philosophical defense of the Christian doctrine of God as Three in One. His *Plea on Behalf of Christians* was addressed to the emperors Hadrian and Antoninus.

Chapter 1

A Destiny Beyond Dust

ALFRED TENNYSON—1850

Strong Son of God, immortal Love,
    Whom we, that have not seen thy face,
    By faith, and faith alone, embrace,
Believing where we cannot prove;

Thine are these orbs of light and shade;
    Thou madest Life in man and brute;
    Thou madest Death; and lo, thy foot
Is on the skull which thou hast made.

Thou wilt not leave us in the dust:
    Thou madest man, he knows not why;
    He thinks he was not made to die;
And thou hast made him: thou art just.

Thou seemest human and divine,
    The highest, holiest manhood, thou:
    Our wills are ours, we know not how;
Our wills are ours, to make them thine.

Our little systems have their day;
    They have their day and cease to be:
    They are but broken lights of thee,
And thou, O Lord, art more than they.

We have but faith: we cannot know;
    For knowledge is of things we see;
    And yet we trust it comes from thee,
A beam in darkness: let it grow.

ALFRED TENNYSON (1809–1892) is often regarded as the chief representative of the Victorian age in poetry. Son of a clergyman, he was tutored at home and then studied at Trinity College, Cambridge. He was appointed poet laureate by Queen Victoria in 1850, succeeding Wordsworth. He held the title for forty-two years and was buried in the Poets' Corner in Westminster Abbey. Tennyson's works tended toward the melancholic, reflecting the moral and intellectual values of England in his time.

It Is Going to Be All Right

JOHN BAILLIE—TWENTIETH CENTURY

NOT EVEN THE MOST learned philosopher or theologian knows what it is going to be like. But there is one thing which the simplest Christian knows—it is going to be all right. Somewhere, somewhen, somehow we who are worshiping God here will wake up to see Him as He is, and face to face. No doubt it will all be utterly different from anything we have ever imagined or thought about it. No doubt God Himself will be unimaginably different from all our present conceptions of Him. But He will be unimaginably different only because He will be unimaginably better. The only thing we do certainly know is that our highest hopes will be more than fulfilled, and our deepest longings more than gratified.

JOHN BAILLIE (1886–1960) was a Scottish theologian and professor at the University of Edinburgh. Ecumenical in his vision, he also served as president of the World Council of Churches. He had a deep concern for the doubts people might have regarding the Christian faith and excelled as an apologist. His most famous devotional work is the widely circulated *A Diary of Private Prayer.*

Chapter 1

The Signature of the Soul

C. S. Lewis—1962

We are very shy nowadays of even mentioning heaven. We are afraid of the jeer about "pie in the sky," and of being told that we are trying to "escape" from the duty of making a happy world here and now into dreams of a happy world elsewhere. But either there is "pie in the sky" or there is not. If there is not, then Christianity is false, for this doctrine is woven into its whole fabric. If there is, then this truth, like any other, must be faced, whether it is useful at political meetings or no. Again, we are afraid that heaven is a bribe, and that if we make it our goal we shall no longer be disinterested. It is not so. Heaven offers nothing that a mercenary soul can desire. It is safe to tell the pure in heart that they shall see God, for only the pure in heart want to. There are rewards that do not sully motives. A man's love for a woman is not mercenary because he wants to marry her, nor his love for poetry mercenary because he wants to read it, nor his love of exercise less disinterested because he wants to run and leap and walk. Love, by definition, seeks to enjoy its object.

You may think that there is another reason for our silence about heaven—namely, that we do not really desire it. But that may be an illusion. What I am now going to say is merely an opinion of my own without the slightest authority, which I submit to the judgement of better Christians and better scholars than myself. There have been times when I think we do not desire heaven but more often I find myself wondering whether, in our heart of hearts, we have ever desired anything else. You may have noticed that the books you really love are bound together by a secret thread. You know very well what is the common quality that makes you love them, though you cannot put it into words: but most of your friends do not see it at all, and often wonder why, liking this, you should also like that. Again, you have stood before some landscape, which seems to embody what you have been looking for all your life; and then turned to the friend at your side who appears to be seeing what you saw—but at the first words a gulf yawns between you, and you realise that this landscape means something totally different to him, that he is pursuing an alien vision and cares nothing for the ineffable suggestion by which you are transported. Even in your hobbies, has there not always been some secret attraction which the others are curiously ignorant of—something, not to be identified with, but always on the verge of breaking through, the smell of cut wood in the workshop or the clap-clap of water against the boat's side? Are not all lifelong friendships born at the moment when at last you meet another human being who has some inkling (but faint and uncertain even in the best) of that something which you were born desiring, and which, beneath the flux of other desires and in all the momentary silences between the louder passions, night and day, year by year, from childhood to old age, you are looking for, watching for, listening for? You have never *had* it. All the things that have ever deeply possessed your soul have been but hints of it—tantalising glimpses, promises never quite fulfilled, echoes that died away just as they caught your ear. But if it should really become manifest—if there ever came an echo that did not die away but swelled into the sound itself—you would know it. Beyond all possibility of doubt you would say, "Here at last is the thing I was made for." We cannot tell each other about it. It is the secret signature of each soul, the incommunicable and unappeasable want, the thing we desired before we met our wives or made our friends or chose our work, and which we shall still desire on our deathbeds, when the mind no longer knows wife or friend or work. While we are, this is. If we lose this, we lose all.

All that you are, sins apart, is destined, if you will let God have His good way, to utter satisfaction.

This signature on each soul may be a product of heredity and environment, but that only means that heredity and environment are among the instruments whereby God creates a soul. I am considering not how, but why, He makes each soul unique. If He had no use for all these differences, I do not see why He should have created more souls than one. Be sure that the ins and outs of your individuality are no mystery to Him; and one day they will no longer be a mystery to you. The mould in which a key is made would be a strange thing, if you had never seen a key: and the key itself a strange thing if you had never seen a lock. Your soul has a curious shape because it is a hollow made to fit a particular swelling in the infinite contours of the divine substance, or a key to unlock one of the doors in the house with many mansions. For it is not humanity in the abstract that is to be saved, but you—you, the individual reader, John Stubbs or Janet Smith. Blessed and fortunate creature, your eyes shall behold Him and not another's. All that you are, sins apart, is destined, if you will let God have His good way, to utter satisfaction. The Brocken spectre "looked to every man like his first love" because she was a cheat. But God will look to every soul like its first love because He is its first love. Your place in heaven will seem to be made for you and you alone, because you were made for it—made for it stitch by stitch as a glove is made for a hand.

C. S. Lewis (1898–1963) taught medieval and renaissance literature at the universities of Oxford and Cambridge. He is known as a brilliant scholar and an apologist for the Christian faith, and his writings have been popular and influential well beyond the boundaries of academia.

Heaven Beckons, and Baffles

Emily Dickinson — *circa* 1862

This World is not Conclusion.
A Species stands beyond—
Invisible, as Music—
But positive, as Sound—
It beckons, and it baffles—
Philosophy—don't know—
And through a Riddle, at the last—
Sagacity, must go—
To guess it, puzzles scholars—
To gain it, Men have borne
Contempt of Generations
And Crucifixion, shown—

Faith slips—and laughs, and rallies—
Blushes, if any see—
Plucks at a twig of Evidence—
And asks a Vane, the way—
Much Gesture, from the Pulpit—
Strong Hallelujahs roll—
Narcotics cannot still the Tooth
That nibbles at the soul—

EMILY DICKINSON (1830–1886) was born in Amherst, Massachusetts, where her grandfather had been a founder of Amherst College and her father was its treasurer. Except for a year spent at Mount Holyoke Female Seminary in South Hadley, Massachusetts, she lived in Amherst her entire life, never marrying, and confining herself mostly to her home. Emily Dickinson wrote more than 1,700 poems, only seven of which were published during her lifetime. Today her body of poetry is regarded as among the best in the English language, and the Dickinson home in Amherst is a tourist mecca.

To Die Is Gain

R. C. SPROUL—1988

BLAISE PASCAL once observed that a crucial element of man's misery is found in this: He can always contemplate a better life than it is possible for him to achieve. We all have the ability to dream, to allow our imaginations to soar in free flight of fancy. Yet when we push our imaginative powers to their limit, we crash into the barrier of the unknown. Who can imagine what heaven is really like? It is beyond our ken. It is beyond our most ambitious dreams.

One sage remarked that if we could imagine the most pleasant experience possible and thought about doing it for eternity, we would be conceiving of something that would be closer to hell than to heaven. We simply cannot fathom a situation of absolute felicity. We have no concrete reference point for it. . . .

It is the unknown quality of the afterlife that makes us rather bear those ills we have than fly to others we know not of. . . . Not only do we have the ability to contemplate a better existence than we presently enjoy; we also have the power to imagine a worse existence than we presently endure.

Our imaginings about the afterlife are restricted primarily to analogy. To move beyond this world is to move into another dimension. That different dimension involves both continuity and discontinuity. Insofar as there is continuity we can think by way of analogies drawn from this world. The elements of discontinuity remain inscrutable. We simply cannot grasp what goes beyond our points of reference.

Though the Bible is somewhat oblique about our future state, it is not altogether silent. We are given hints, vital clues about what heaven is like. There is a kind of tantalizing foretaste of future glory that is set before us. There is a partial unveiling that gives us a glimpse behind the dark glass. . . .

Paul speaks of death as *gain*. We tend to think of death as *loss*. To be sure, the death of a loved one involves a loss for those who are left behind. But for the one who passes from this world to heaven it is gain.

Paul does not despise life in this world. He says that he is "hard pressed" between choosing to remain and desiring to depart. The contrast he points to between this life and heaven is not a contrast between the bad and the good. The comparison is between the *good* and the *better*. This life in Christ is good. Life in heaven is better. Yet he takes it a step farther. He declares that to depart and be with Christ is *far better* (Philippians 1:23). The transition to heaven involves more than a slight or marginal improvement. The gain is great. Heaven is far better than life in this world.

R. C. Sproul holds degrees from Westminster College, Pittsburgh Theological Seminary, the Free University of Amsterdam, Geneva College, and Grove City College. He is the founder and chairman of Ligonier Ministries, has taught at numerous colleges and seminaries, is currently a pastor, and has written many books. He is known for tackling difficult topics and expounding them well.

Heaven over Us

CHRISTINA GEORGINA ROSSETTI — *circa* 1893

Heaven overarches earth and sea,
    Earth-sadness and sea-bitterness.
Heaven overarches you and me:
A little while and we shall be—
Please God—where there is no more sea
    Nor barren wilderness.
Heaven overarches you and me,
    And all earth's gardens and her graves.
Look up with me, until we see
The day break and the shadows flee.
What though to-night wrecks you and me,
    If so to-morrow saves?

CHRISTINA GEORGINA ROSSETTI (1840–1894), sister of painter Dante Gabriel Rossetti, was numbered among the Pre-Raphaelites, a group of English poets and painters who sought to imitate the simplicity of medieval styles in protest against the materialism of an industrial society. Christina never married, and her poetry was filled with themes of death and the renunciation of earthly love. She was a devout Anglican.

They Wait for Us

CYPRIAN — 252

IF IN YOUR DWELLING the walls were shaking with age, the roofs above you were trembling, and the house, now worn out and wearied, were threatening an immediate destruction to its structure crumbling with age, would you not with all speed depart? If, when you were on a voyage, an angry and raging tempest, by the waves violently aroused, foretold the coming shipwreck, would you not quickly seek the harbour? Lo, the world is changing and passing away, and witnesses to its ruin not now by its age, but by the end of things. And do you not give God thanks, do you not congratulate yourself, that by an earlier departure you are taken away, and delivered from the shipwrecks and disasters that are imminent?

What a pleasure is there in the heavenly kingdom, without fear of death; and how lofty and perpetual a happiness with eternity of living!

We should consider, dearly beloved brethren—we should ever and anon reflect that we have renounced the world, and are in the meantime living here as guests and strangers. Let us greet the day which assigns each of us to his own home, which snatches us hence, and sets us free from the snares of the world, and restores us to paradise and the kingdom. Who that has been placed in foreign lands would not hasten to return to his own country? Who that is hastening to return to his friends would not eagerly desire a prosperous gale, that he might the sooner embrace those dear to him? We regard paradise as our country—we already begin to consider the patriarchs as our parents: why do we not hasten and run, that we may behold our country, that we may greet our parents? There a great number of our dear ones is awaiting us, and a dense crowd of parents, brothers, children, is longing for us, already assured of their own safety, and still solicitous for our salvation. To attain to their presence and their embrace, what a gladness both for them and for us in common! What a pleasure is there in the heavenly kingdom, without fear of death; and how lofty and perpetual a happiness with eternity of living! There the glorious company of the apostles—there the host of the rejoicing prophets—there the innumerable multitude of martyrs, crowned for the victory of their struggle and passion—there the triumphant virgins, who subdued the lust of the flesh and of the body by the strength of their continency—there are merciful men rewarded, who by feeding and helping the poor have done the works of righteousness—who, keeping the Lord's precepts, have transferred their earthly patrimonies to the heavenly treasuries. To these, beloved brethren, let us hasten with an eager desire; let us crave quickly to be with them, and quickly to come to Christ. May God behold this our eager desire; may the Lord Christ look upon this purpose of our mind and faith, He who will give the larger rewards of His glory to those whose desires in respect of Himself were greater!

CYPRIAN (200–258), or THASCIUS CAECILIANUS CYPRIANUS, was a teacher of rhetoric who converted to Christianity around 246. He quickly mastered the Scriptures, and was soon elected bishop of Carthage. He was exiled from Carthage during the persecution under the emperor Decius and was later martyred in the persecution under Valerian. He organized works of charity and opposed the easy readmittance of Christians who had yielded to persecution and sacrificed to the emperor.

The Distant Voices

ANNA SHIPTON—1857

Nearer and nearer day by day the distant voices come;
Soft through the pearly gate they swell, and seem to call me
home.
The lamp of life burns faint and low; ay; let it fainter burn;
For who would weep the failing lamp when birds announce
the morn?
I saw the faces of my loved gleam through the twilight dim,
And softly on the morning air arose the heaven-born hymn.
With looks of love they gazed on me, as none gaze on me now;
The glory of the Infinite surrounded every brow.
Fair lilies, star-like in their bloom, and waving palms they
bore,
And oh, the smiles of peace and joy those heavenly faces wore!
Thou who hast fathomed death's dark tide, save me from
death's alarms;
Beneath my trembling soul, oh, stretch Thine everlasting
arms!

No second cross, no thorny crown can bruise Thy sacred
brow;
Thou who the wine-press trod alone, o'er the dark wave bear
me now.
A parting hour, a pang of pain, and then shall pass away
The veil that shrouds Thee where Thou reign'st in everlasting
day.
No sin, no sigh, no withering fear, can wring the bosom there;
But basking in Thy smile I shall Thy sinless service share.
How long, O Lord, how long before Thou'lt take me by the
hand,
And I, Thy weakest child, at last among Thy children stand?
Beyond the stars that steadfast shine my spirit pines to soar,
To dwell within my Father's house, and leave that home no
more.
O Lord, Thou hast with angel food my fainting spirit fed;
If 'tis Thy will I linger here, bless Thou the path I tread;
And though my soul doth pant to pass within the pearly gate,
Yet teach me for Thy summons, Lord, in patience still to wait.

Anna Shipton (d. 1901) lived in England during the mid-to-late nineteenth century and published several volumes of devotional poetry and other books. Though little remembered today, she was a popular writer in her lifetime, and her *Whispers in the Palms* went through at least five editions. C. H. Spurgeon used her verses in a hymnbook published for his Metropolitan Tabernacle, and D. L. Moody was fond of quoting her poetry.

A Parable of Immortality

Henry Van Dyke—*circa* 1911

I am standing upon the seashore. A ship at my side spreads her white sails to the morning breeze and starts for the blue ocean. She is an object of beauty and strength, and I stand and watch her

until at length she hangs like a speck of white cloud just where
the sea and sky come down to mingle with each other.
Then someone at my side says "There! She's gone."
Gone where? Gone from my sight—that is all.
She is just as large in mast and hull and spar as she was
when she left my side, and just as able to bear her load
of living freight to the place of destination. Her diminished
size is in me, not in her; and just at the moment when
someone at my side says, "There! She's gone," there are
other eyes watching her coming, and other voices ready to
take up the glad shout, "There she comes!"
And that is Dying!

Henry Van Dyke (1852–1933) was an American author, educator, and clergyman. He graduated from Princeton University in 1873 and from Princeton Theological Seminary in 1874, and served as a professor of English literature at Princeton between 1899 and 1923, with some notable time away: From 1908 to 1909 Dr. Van Dyke was American lecturer at the University of Paris. In 1913, by appointment of President Woodrow Wilson, he became an ambassador, the Minister to the Netherlands and Luxembourg. He was also a U.S. Navy chaplain before returning to teaching at Princeton in 1918. Among his popular writings is the Christmas story *The Other Wise Man* (1896). Various religious themes are also expressed in his poetry, hymns, and essays collected in *Little Rivers* (1895) and *Fisherman's Luck* (1899).

Longing for Home

Don Piper—2000

Without the slightest doubt, I know heaven *is* real. It's more real than anything I've ever experienced in my life. I sometimes say, "Think of the worst thing that's ever happened to you, and everything in between; heaven is more real than any of those things."

Since my return to earth, I've been acutely aware that all of us are on a pilgrimage. At the end of this life, wherever we go—heaven or hell—life will be more real than this one we're now living.

I never thought of that before my accident, of course. Heaven was a concept, something I believed in, but didn't think about it often.

In the years since my accident, I've repeatedly thought of the last night Jesus was with his disciples before his betrayal and crucifixion. Only hours before he began that journey to heaven, he sat with his disciples in the upper room. He begged them not to be troubled and to trust in him. Then he told them he was going away and added, "In my Father's house are many rooms; if it were not so, I would have told you. I am going there to prepare a place for you. And if I go and prepare a place for you, I will come back and take you to be with me that you also may be where I am" (John 14:2–3).

I had never really noticed it before, but twice Jesus used the word *place*—a location. Perhaps that may not stir most people, but I think about it often. It is a literal place, and I can testify that I know that place. I've been there. I know heaven is real.

Since my accident, I've felt more intensely and deeply than ever before. A year in a hospital bed can do that for anyone, but it was more than just that. Those ninety minutes in heaven left such an impression on me that I can never be the same person I was. I can never again be totally content here, because I live in anticipation.

Don Piper is a minister of education and single adults at the First Baptist Church in Pasadena, Texas. He regularly appears on Christian television and radio programs, writes a weekly newspaper column, and leads conferences and retreats in the United States and abroad.

Passage to Heaven

Joseph Bayly—1977

I'm ashamed to admit it, but I'm a little scared.
I really like this world: the Rocky Mountains,

the beach at Cape May, the fields behind our house,
the barn through mist on a gray wintry morning.
How can I adjust to heaven when it's so different?
  That world you like,
  it is but a womb.
A womb?
  Yes, you may not
  perceive it that way
  but you are bound within
  earthworld as surely as a baby yet
  unborn is bound
  within the womb
    The death incident is merely a passage from earth life,
    from the womb that has contained you until now, into
      the marvelous newness of heaven life.
Maybe the baby
would be scared to be born,
to leave the womb.
  Then death is . . .
  deliverance to life beyond your imagining
    The death incident is merely a passage from earth life,
    from the womb that has contained you until now, into
    the marvelous newness of heaven life. You'll go
    through a dark tunnel, you may experience pain—
    just as you did when you were born a baby—but
    beyond the tunnel is heaven.
    I promise you, you'll enjoy heaven.

Joseph Bayly graduated from Wheaton College and Faith Seminary. After a long career as an author, educator, editor, and ultimately president of a Christian publishing company, he went to the heaven he loved to describe. He is remembered as a noted Christian leader.

Chapter 1

Looking Forward to Heaven's Joy

J. I. PACKER—1977

EVERLASTING LIFE is something to which I look forward. Why? Not because I am out of love with life here—just the reverse! My life is full of joy, from four sources—knowing God, and people, and the good and pleasant things that God and men under God have created, and doing things which are worthwhile for God or others, or for myself as God's man. But my reach exceeds my grasp. My relationships with God and others are never as rich and full as I want them to be, and I am always finding more than I thought was there in great music, great verse, great books, great lives, and the great kaleidoscope of the natural order. . . .

As I get older, I find that I appreciate God, and people, and good and lovely and noble things, more and more intensely; so it is pure delight to think that this enjoyment will continue and increase in some form (what form, God knows, and I am content to wait and see), literally forever. Christians inherit in fact the destiny that fairy tales envisage in fancy: we (yes, you and I, the silly saved sinners) live, and live happily, and by God's endless mercy will live happily ever after.

We cannot visualize heaven's life, and the wise man will not try. Instead, we will dwell on the doctrine of heaven, which is that there the redeemed will find all their heart's desire: joy with their Lord, joy with His people, and joy in the ending of all frustration and distress and the supply of all wants. . . .

Often now we say in moments of great enjoyment, "I don't want this ever to stop"—but it does. Heaven, however, is different. May heaven's joy be yours, and mine.

J. I. PACKER is professor of theology at Regent College in Vancouver, British Columbia, and the author of numerous books, including *Knowing God,* that many consider contemporary classics.

Life's Octave

JOHN HYDE CLEGHORN—1995

Before a sound was ever heard,
  There always was th' eternal Word.
The flow of Time was a formless jam,
  Without the hand of the Great I Am.
Man's groping power's of no avail,
  A puff of air in celestial gale.
We rest serene in micro-space,
  Wombed in God's unbounded Grace.
The time will come, we always know,
  Relentless change—our time to go.
Fear gives way in selfless tide,
  Of urge to peer at the other side.
God gives us charts, a timeless Book,
  Our minds reach out, an eager look.
We see the joy, Faith's free reward,
  Timeless life with a Risen Lord!

JOHN HYDE CLEGHORN (1909–1996) was a graduate of the University of the South. His career was in radio and advertising/public relations. However, his avocations were soloist, Bible teacher, and wordsmith.

It's Going to Be Wonderful

JONI EARECKSON TADA—2003

HEAVEN IS TOO WONDERFUL FOR WORDS. I can't describe it. It would be like asking a caterpillar about flying, like asking a flower bulb what [it] is like to be fragrant, or like asking a coconut, all hard and hairy, what it is like to be swaying in the breeze and be all tall and beautiful. A coconut can't imagine that. A caterpillar can't imagine flying. A bulb can't ever imagine what it is to be fragrant.

A peach pit has no concept what it means to bear fruit and give shade and be delightful. And yet within each of those little things is that seed, that identity, of what one day it will become, of what one day it is destined to be. Somewhere within me is this seed of what one day I am destined to be. What I will be then is who I am now. The pattern of it is somehow within me, but I cannot even begin to imagine it. I have just got a coconut brain, like a flower bulb trying to think fragrance.

Joni Eareckson Tada, having been tutored in God's Word amidst the bruising reality of quadriplegia for over thirty years, is the author of over twenty books dealing with God's hand in hardship. She is the founder and president of Joni and Friends, a disability outreach ministry.

CHAPTER 2

The Glory of Heaven

A Dazzling Sight

MATTHEW PRIOR—*circa* 1700

As through the artist's intervening glass
Our eyes observe the distant planets pass;
A little we discover, but allow
That more remains unseen than art can show:
So whilst our mind its knowledge would improve
(Its feeble eye intent on things above),
High as we may lift our reason up,
By faith directed, and confirmed by hope:
Yet we are able only to survey
Dawnings of beams, and promises of day.
Heaven's fuller effluence mocks our dazzled sight:
Too great its swiftness, and too strong its light:
But soon the 'mediate clouds shall be dispelled;
The sun shall then be face to face beheld,
In all his robes, with all his glory on,
Seated sublime on his meridian throne.

MATTHEW PRIOR (1664–1721), of London, was educated at Cambridge and then held various diplomatic posts, as well as serving as a member of Parliament. He is best known today for his satirical or humorous poetry, some of which he wrote while in prison for political reasons.

Chapter 2

The Brilliance of Heaven

John F. MacArthur—1996

There will be no need of cosmic light sources. Revelation 21:23 says, "The city had no need of the sun, neither of the moon, to shine in it: for the glory of God did lighten it, and the Lamb is the light thereof" (KJV).

The glory of heaven is a far more brilliant light than the light of the sun. In fact, Isaiah wrote, "Then the moon will be abashed and the sun ashamed, for the Lord of hosts will reign on Mount Zion and in Jerusalem, and His glory will be before His elders" (24:23 NASB). Next to the glory of God, the light of the sun and moon are paltry, flickering candles. Revelation 21:24 adds that "the nations shall walk by its light, and the kings of the earth shall bring their glory into it" (NASB). John is saying that even the kings of the earth will yield up their own glory in the face of the glory of heaven. All nations will walk in the light of God's presence, and all men, regardless of their position, will bow to His glory. . . .

In heaven we will actually see the Lord face to face. This is impossible in the earthly realm. After all, God said, "No man can see Me and live!" (Exodus 33:20 NASB). John 1:18 and 1 John 4:12 both say, "No man hath seen God at any time" (KJV). First Timothy 6:16 declares that God "alone possesses immortality and dwells in unapproachable light; whom no man has seen or can see" (NASB). Indeed, God is "of purer eyes than to behold evil, and [cannot] look on iniquity" (Habakkuk 1:13 KJV). As long as we are tainted by sin, we cannot see God. The view of such perfect righteousness would destroy us.

God is therefore inaccessible to mortal man on a face-to-face basis. This is what made Christ's incarnation so wonderful: although no man has ever seen God at any time, "the only begotten Son, which is in the bosom of the Father, he hath declared him" (John 1:18). Christ "dwelt among us (and we beheld his glory, the glory as of the only begotten of the Father)" (John 1:14). He came to our world to dwell among us, and He did it in order to redeem us and take us to heaven, where Father, Son, and Holy Spirit will dwell in our midst in perfect fellowship. What a breathtaking reality!

In heaven, since we will be free from sin, we will see God's glory unveiled in its fullness. That will be a more pleasing, spectacular sight than anything we have known or could ever imagine on earth. No mere earthly pleasure can even begin to measure up to the privilege and the ecstasy of an unhindered view of the divine glory. . . .

We will bask in the glory of God, realizing at last our chief end—to glorify God and to *enjoy* Him forever. The psalmist wrote, "In thy presence is fullness of joy; at thy right hand there are pleasures for evermore" (Psalm 16:11 KJV).

Scripture repeatedly makes clear that heaven is a realm of unsurpassed joy, unfading glory, undiminished bliss, unlimited delights, and unending pleasures.

Such a thought is unfathomable to our finite minds. But Scripture repeatedly makes clear that heaven is a realm of unsurpassed joy, unfading glory, undiminished bliss, unlimited delights, and unending pleasures. Nothing about it can possibly be boring or humdrum. It will be a perfect existence.

JOHN F. MACARTHUR is pastor-teacher of Grace Community Church in Sun Valley, California, president of The Master's College and Seminary, and featured teacher with the Grace to You media ministry. His popular expository style of teaching is evident in his numerous bestselling books.

The Glory of Paradise

PETER DAMIANI—ELEVENTH CENTURY

To the fount of life eternal cries the soul with longing thirst,
And the spirit, flesh-imprisoned, seeks the bars of flesh to
burst;
Strives to gain that heavenly country, exiled now and sin-
accurst.

Sore beset with care and danger, groans the spirit for release,
Still beholds, though lost in Eden, glory forfeited and peace;
Former good, in memory dwelling, doth the present ill increase.
Who can tell how great the joy of that Peace surpassing all,
Where of living pearls constructed rise the stately buildings tall,
Where with gold the rooftree glitters, shines with gold the banquet-hall.

All of precious stones compacted rise those structures of delight,
Purest gold as crystal shining paves the heavenly city bright;
Never mire nor filth defiling stains the streets of radiant light.

Chilling winter, burning summer, neither rages in that land,
But the crimson bloom of roses doth an endless spring demand;
White the lilies, red the crocus, fragrant doth the balsam stand.

Green the pastures, flower-besprinkled, fed by streams with honey filled;
All the air is sweet with incense from the odorous herbs distilled;
Never falls the ripened fruitage, nor is bloom by winter chilled.

Waxeth not the moon nor waneth, need not sun or stars to be,
But the Lamb in that blest City shines a Sun eternally:
There the daylight is unbroken, night and time have ceased to be.

Shine the blessed with a splendor like the splendor of the sun;
Crowned in triumph stand they singing that the race of life is run;
Now secure, they count the glories of the contest they have won.

Cleansed from every stain of evil, they from carnal strife are free;
Flesh made spirit, with the spirit doth for evermore agree:
There, released from all affliction, they shall Peace unbroken see.

Stripped of changing accidentals, they the changeless source attain;
Truth unveiled and beatific they to gaze upon shall gain;
Living sweetness from the waters of the living fountain drain.

Thus they reach a state unchanging, undisturbed and permanent,
Filled with life and joy of living, subject not to accident;
To the strong, the ever youthful, nor is age nor illness sent.

Here possess they life eternal, passing things have passed away;
Here they bloom, they thrive, they flourish; vanquished now is all decay;
Clothed with life's immortal vigor, death for them hath lost his sway.

Knowing well the Source of all things, naught there is they cannot know;
Every secret penetrating, which was hid from them below;
Unity of thought and purpose, perfect unity they show.

Granted that the prize be varied, and with toil commensurate,
What in others love desireth, love doth this appropriate;
Thus the common good combineth what in each was separate.

As around a victim body circling eagles congregate,
There do holy souls, with angels, all their hunger ever sate;
One the Living Bread they feed on, citizens of either state.

Ever filled, yet ever eager, need and appetite agree;
Hunger brings not torment with it, plenty not satiety:
Ever eager for the feasting, ever feast they eagerly.

Ever more the voice melodic makes new harmonies to ring;
Instruments of heavenly music their exultant concord bring;
Worthy of the King who saves them are the praises that they sing.

Blest the soul that contemplates thee, King of Heaven, face to face,
And beneath her sees revolving the concentric orbs in space,
Sees the sun, the moon, the planets all their two-fold journey trace.

Christ, the palm of worthy warriors, when my sword is laid aside,
Bring me to thy heavenly City, there for ever to abide,
Grant that I the veteran's bounty with thy faithful may divide.

Strength supply, in heat of conflict, ceaseless struggle to maintain;
Grant thy servant, warfare ended, well-deserved rest to gain;
Grant that I, thyself deserving, may thyself as prize attain!

PETER DAMIANI (1001–1072), a teacher of Ravenna, Italy, became a Benedictine monk in the monastery of Fonte Avellana. Pope Stephen IX named him cardinal bishop of Ostia in 1057. His fame spread as he took a leading role in the moral revival of the church instigated by Pope Gregory VII. After returning to monastic life, Peter Damiani wrote unceasingly on theological and devotional topics and composed poetry. His *Song on the Joy and Glory of Paradise* was included in a medieval collection of meditations falsely attributed to Augustine of Hippo, but its true authorship ultimately came to light.

The Shining Glory of God

DR. TONY EVANS—2000

SINCE WE'RE TRYING TO IMAGINE the unimaginable, think about what heaven must look like with the undiminished glory of God continuously illuminating all the layers or tiers of this crystal-clear, transparent city.

Here's one more thing to consider. The New Jerusalem is not only designed to let God's glory shine through; it is designed to reflect His glory from every part of the city. So when God's glory hits the street, it will be reflected off the street to the wall. And when God's glory hits the wall, it will bounce off the wall.

In other words, everywhere you go in heaven you will be totally surrounded by God's glory! What a staggering concept. What an awe-inspiring place heaven will be.

Heaven is not only perfect in its beauty, but it is every preacher's dream because it is a place of perfect worship.

During his vision of heaven, John wrote, "I heard a loud voice from the throne, saying, 'Behold, the tabernacle of God is among men, and He shall dwell among them, and they shall be His people, and God Himself shall be among them'" (Revelation 21:3).

The tabernacle in the Old Testament served the same basic purpose as the church in the New Testament. It was the place where people went to worship God, whether New Testament believers met in the temple or in a private house.

Since heaven itself is God's temple, every place we go, everything we do, and every conversation we have will be an act of worship.

One reason we need to go to church is to be reminded of God. Satan tries to make us forget God the minute we walk out of the church doors on Sunday, and all week long we are engaged in a spiritual battle with an Enemy who wants to blot God from our memory.

But in heaven there will be no tabernacle or temple (Revelation

21:22), no place we need to go to be reminded of God. It's not necessary, because heaven is permeated by the all-consuming presence of God. You won't need to go to church in heaven, because you will be surrounded by and engulfed in His presence.

I can hear someone saying, "You mean we are going to be in church all day long every day?" *It's Sunday. Gotta go to church again.* I know some people feel that way when Sunday morning comes around. But anyone who feels that way doesn't understand worship. Worship was never meant to be an exercise held in a building once a week. Paul stated the essence of worship when he said, "Whether, then, you eat or drink or whatever you do, do all to the glory of God" (1 Corinthians 10:31). True worship is every area of our lives reflecting the true glory of God.

So the issue isn't whether you are in church all day in heaven. It's that everything you are and do throughout eternity will reflect who and what God is and bring Him eternal glory. That's worship.

Since heaven itself is God's temple, every place we go, everything we do, and every conversation we have will be an act of worship.

This is worship as it was meant to be.

We will live in God's reflected glory all the time, and there will never be a moment when His presence doesn't impact us. We will never feel distant from God, or alone or cut off from Him. Heaven will be pure, eternal worship.

TONY EVANS is a pastor of Oak Cliff Fellowship, Dallas, Texas, and president of The Urban Alternative, a teaching ministry targeting the inner city. He is the author of numerous books, including *Returning to Your First Love, The Battle Is the Lord's,* and *No More Excuses*.

Our Everlasting Light

WILLIAM COWPER—1779

Hear what God the Lord hath spoken,
"O my people, faint and few;

Comfortless, afflicted, broken,
Fair abodes I build for you;
Thorns of heart-felt tribulation
Shall no more perplex your ways;
You shall name your walls, Salvation,
And your gates shall all be praise.

"There, like streams that feed the garden,
Pleasures, without end, shall flow:
For the Lord, your faith rewarding,
All his bounty shall bestow:
Still in undisturb'd possession
Peace and righteousness shall reign;
Never shall you feel oppression,
Hear the voice of war again.

"Ye no more your suns descending,
Waning moons no more shall see;
But, your griefs for ever ending,
Find eternal noon in me:
God shall rise, and shining o'er you,
Change to day the gloom of night;
He, the Lord, shall be your glory,
God your everlasting light."

William Cowper (1731–1800), born in Hertfordshire, England, studied to become an attorney but never practiced law. He experienced depression and had several attacks of mental illness. Having become intensely devout through his illness, he worked as an assistant to John Newton, author of "Amazing Grace." Newton encouraged Cowper to write hymns, and together they published *Olney Hymns,* named for the town in Buckinghamshire where they resided. His most famous hymn is "God Moves in a Mysterious Way," originally titled "Light Shining out of Darkness."

Chapter 2

The Shining Being

RANDY ALCORN—1996

AT THE DOORWAY INTO LIFE stood a shining being of natural radiance, but with the brightness of a million klieg lights. The radiance threatened to blind her, but somehow her new eyes could endure it. This was more than a man, yet clearly a man. She knew at once who it was. He who had been from eternity past, he who had left his home in heaven to make one here for her. He who spun the galaxies into being with a single snap of his fingers, who was the light that illumined darkness with a million colors, who turned midnight into sunrise.

It was he. Not his representative, but he himself. He put his hands upon her shoulders and she thrilled at his touch.

"Welcome, my little one!" He smiled broadly, the smile teeming with approval. "Well done, my good and faithful servant. Enter into the kingdom prepared for you. Enter into the joy of your Lord!"

He hugged her tight and she hugged him back, clutching on to his back, then grasping his shoulders. She didn't know how long it lasted. These same arms had hugged her before, somehow—she recognized their character and strength—but she enjoyed the embrace now as she'd never dreamed she could enjoy any embrace. It was complete, utterly encompassing, a wall of protection no force in the universe could break through. His was the embrace she was made for. He was the Bridegroom, the object of all longing, the fulfillment of all dreams.

"My sweet Jesus," she said.

She bowed to worship him and he delighted in her worship. Then he lifted her up effortlessly and gazed into her eyes. She studied his eyes through the blur. She saw in them things she had long known coupled with things she had never imagined and still others she sensed she would never fully grasp.

"You're crying," he said. He put out his hand and wiped away her tears. As the hand came close to her cheek a feeling of terror struck her, a feeling she'd assumed could have no place here in Joy itself. She cringed because she saw his outstretched hand was marred and disfigured.

"Your hand." She looked at the other. "Both hands. And your feet." He allowed her to contemplate what she saw.

Hands and feet of the only innocent man became forever scarred so that no guilty one would have to bear his own scars.

These were the hands of a Carpenter who cut wood and made things, including universes and angels and every person who had ever lived. These same hands once hauled heavy lumber up a long lonely hill. These same hands and feet were once nailed to that lumber in the Shadowlands, in the most terrible moment from the dawn of time. The wound that healed all wounds could make them temporary only by making itself eternal. Hands and feet of the only innocent man became forever scarred so that no guilty one would have to bear his own scars.

She saw his pain. An ancient pain that was the doorway to eternal pleasures.

Understanding rushed upon her and penetrated her mind as the howling wind had penetrated every crack in her bedroom in that old ramshackle Mississippi home. She wept again, dropping to his mangled feet and caressing them with her hands. He put his fingers under her chin and turned her eyes up toward his.

"For you," he said to her, "I would do it all again."

She could not stop weeping. She was surprised she could cry here, one of the first surprises in an eternity that would bring endless ones. If some tears would never be cried again, she thought, then tears of love and joy and fulfillment were among heaven's pleasures.

She searched the Carpenter's face as one searches a face she has yearned for, which she has seen in her dreams as long as she can remember. On the right side of his throat, she saw another scar, a mark of discoloration, not prominent, only an inch long. The scar looked remarkably like . . . She reached suddenly to the side of her neck to feel the scar from the broken beer bottle. She couldn't feel it. Gone.

He smiled at her, rubbing his finger on his scar, which used to be hers, just as she had so often done on earth. That quickly the scar on his neck disappeared. But the scars on his hands and feet remained. She knew they always would.

They talked long, just the two of them, without hurry and without distraction. A circle of people surrounded them, waiting for them to finish. But she did not want to finish. She was held captive by one face.

Randy Alcorn has dedicated his life to teaching biblical truth and drawing attention to the needy and how to help them. As the founder and director of the nonprofit Eternal Perspective Ministries, Alcorn helps meet the needs of the unreached, unfed, unborn, uneducated, unreconciled, and unsupported people around the world. He is the author of several nonfiction books as well as six novels.

The Heavenly Glory of Christ

Jonathan Edwards—1747

None has ever immediately seen the Father, but the Son; and none else sees the Father any other way, than by the Son's revealing him. And in heaven, the spirits of just men made perfect do see him as he is. They behold his glory. They see the glory of his divine nature, consisting in all the glory of the Godhead, the beauty of all his perfections; his great majesty, almighty power, his infinite wisdom, holiness, and grace, and they see the beauty of his glorified human nature, and the glory which the Father hath given him, as God-man and Mediator. For this end, Christ desired that his saints might "be with him, that they might behold his glory," John xvii. 24. And when the souls of the saints leave their bodies, to go to be with Christ, they behold the marvellous glory of that great work of his, the work of redemption, and of the glorious way of salvation by him. . . . They have a most clear view of the unfathomable depths of the manifold wisdom and knowledge of God; and the most bright displays of the infinite purity and holiness of God, that do appear in that way and work; and see in a much clearer manner than the saints do here, what is the breadth and length, and depth and height of the grace and love of Christ, appearing in his redemption. And as they see the unspeakable riches and glory of the attribute of God's grace, so they most clearly behold and understand Christ's eternal and unmeasurable dying love to them in particular. And in short, they see every thing in Christ that tends to kindle and inflame love, and every thing that tends to gratify love, and every thing that tends to satisfy them: and that in the most clear and glorious manner, without any darkness or delusion, without any impediment or interruption. Now the saints, while in the body, see something of Christ's glory and love; as we, in the dawning of the morning, see something of the reflected light of the sun mingled with darkness; but when separated from the body, they see their glorious and loving Redeemer, as we see the sun when risen, and showing his whole disk above the horizon, by his direct beams, in a clear hemisphere, and with perfect day.

JONATHAN EDWARDS (1703–1758) was a Congregational pastor in Northampton, Massachusetts. His powerful preaching was a factor in the Great Awakening revival of 1734–35, and his sermon "Sinners in the Hands of an Angry God" is one of the most famous examples of American preaching. After his congregation dismissed him because of controversy, he became a missionary to the Indians and was elected president of Princeton University just before his death. He pursued both his preaching and his theological writing with relentless logic, and he has been called "the greatest philosopher-theologian yet to grace the American scene."

The Heavenly Majesty

JOHN BUNYAN—1688

The heavenly Majesty, whose face
Doth far exceed the sun,
Will there cast forth its ray of grace
After this world is done;

Which rays and beams will so possess
 All things that there shall dwell
With so much glory, light, and bliss
 That none can think or tell.

That wisdom which doth order all
 Shall there be fully shown;
That strength that bears the world there shall
 By every one be known.

That holiness and sanctity
 Which doth all thought surpass
Shall there in present purity
 Outshine the crystal glass.

The beauty and the comeliness
 Of this Almighty shall
Make amiable with lasting bliss
 Those he thereto shall call.

The presence of this God will be
 Eternal life in all,
And health and gladness, while we see
 Thy face, O Immortal!

JOHN BUNYAN (1628–1688) of Bedfordshire, England, was not an educated man but a tradesman, a worker in brass. However, his knowledge of the Bible and a few other well-chosen books gave him a mastery of the English language. This led to his formal recognition as an Independent (Congregational) preacher. He was a supporter of the Parliamentary revolution, and after the restoration of the monarchy in 1660 he was imprisoned for most of the following twelve years, during which he began his most sustained writing activity. Bunyan's writings reveal that, to him, the world is a scene of spiritual warfare. *The Pilgrim's Progress,* his best-known work, has been reprinted countless times and translated into more than one hundred languages.

The Glorious Appearing

JONI EARECKSON TADA AND STEVEN ESTES—1997

REMEMBER WHEN WE PEERED into the heavenly whirlwind of joy and pleasure between the Father, Son, and Holy Spirit? Theirs was—or is—a river of joy splashing over heaven's walls onto us. And remember how suffering sandblasts us to the core, removing sin and impurities so that intimacy with Jesus is possible? Do you recall the suffering and the sacrifice Jesus offered that we might know this intimacy and his joy? It was the Savior's mission: "I have told you this so that my joy may be in you" (John 15:11).

Misery may love company, but joy craves a crowd. The Father, Son, and Holy Spirit's plan to rescue humans was not only for man's sake. It is for God's sake. The Father is gathering a crowd—an inheritance, pure and blameless—to worship his Son in the joy of the Holy Spirit. "God is love" (1 John 4:16), and the wish of love is to drench with delight those for whom God has suffered.

Soon the Father, the Son, and the Holy Spirit will get their wish.

Soon, perhaps sooner than we think, "the day of our Lord Jesus Christ" will arrive and "all who have longed for his appearing" will be stripped of the last vestige of sin. God will close the curtain on sin, Satan, and suffering, and we will step into the waterfall of the joy and pleasure that is the Trinity.

Heaven is not a place we are waiting to see; we wait for a Person. It is Jesus we've travailed through all this suffering for.

Better yet, we will become part of a Niagara Falls of thunderous joy as "God is all and in all" for "when he appears we shall be like him for we shall see him as he is." God in us and we in him. No longer will we be "hidden with Christ." "Now we see but a poor reflection; . . . then we shall see face to face. Now I know in part; then I shall know fully, even as I am fully known" (1 Corinthians 13:12)—the apostle Paul who wrote this, who ached to *know* Christ through sharing in the fellowship of his sufferings, will finally get his wish, or *has* his wish now. He is perfectly bonded. Completely united. He not only knows God, he *knows* God in that deep, personal union, that utter euphoria of experiencing him. Paul tasted it in the pain of earth, but now he eats of the "tree of life" in the pleasure of heaven (Revelation 22:2).

Our hope is not a "what," but a "Who." The hope we wait for, our *only* hope, is the "blessed hope—the glorious appearing of our great God and Savior, Jesus Christ" (Titus 2:13). Heaven is not a place we are waiting to see; we wait for a Person. It is Jesus we've travailed through all this suffering for. Our hope is the Desire of the Nations, the Healer of Broken Hearts, the Friend of Sinners. True, we are waiting for the party. But more accurately, we are waiting for the Person who will make it a party.

JONI EARECKSON TADA, having been tutored in God's Word amidst the bruising reality of quadriplegia for over thirty years, is the author of over twenty books dealing with God's hand in hardship. She is founder and president of Joni and Friends, a disability outreach ministry.

STEVEN ESTES holds degrees from Westminster Theological Seminary and Columbia Bible College. He is the senior pastor of Community Evangelical Free Church in Elverson, Pennsylvania. He has co-authored two books with Joni Eareckson Tada.

The Inheritance

GEORGE MACDONALD—1891

SUPPOSE I COULD PERSUADE a man that heaven was the perfection of all he could desire around him, what would the man or the truth gain by it? If he knows the Lord, he will not trouble himself about heaven; if he does not know him, he will not be drawn to *him* by it. I would not care to persuade the feeble Christian that heaven was a place worth going to; I would rather persuade him that no spot in space, no hour in eternity is worth anything to one who remains such as he is.

For my own part, I rejoice to think that there will be neither church nor chapel in the high countries; yea, that there will be nothing there called religion, and no law but the perfect law of liberty. For how should there be law or religion where every throb of the heart says *God!* Where every song-throat is eager with thanksgiving! Where such a tumult of glad waters is for ever bursting from beneath the throne of God, the tears or the gladness of the universe! Religion? Where will be the room for it, when the essence of every thought must be God? Law? What room will there be for law, when everything upon which law could lay a *shall not* will be too loathsome to think of?

Heaven will be continuous touch with God. The very sense of being will in itself be bliss. For the sense of true life, there must be actual, conscious contact with the source of the life; therefore mere life in itself, in its very essence good—good as the life of God which is our life—must be such bliss as, I think, will need the mitigation of the loftiest joys of communion with our blessed fellows; the mitigation of art in every shape, and of all combinations of arts; the mitigation of countless services to the incomplete, and hard toil for those who do not yet know their neighbor or their Father. The bliss of pure being will, I say, need these mitigations to render the intensity of it endurable by heart and brain.

Whatever the place be like, one thing is certain that there will be endless, infinite atonement, ever-growing love. Certain too it is that whatever the divinely human heart desires, it shall not desire in vain. The light which is God, and which is our inheritance because we are the children of God, insures these things. For the heart which desires is made thus to desire. God is; let the earth be glad, and the heaven, and the heaven of heavens! Whatever a father can do to make his children blessed, that will God do for his children. Let us, then, live in continual expectation, looking for the good things that God will give to men, being their Father and their everlasting Savior. If the things I have here come from him, and are so plainly but a beginning, shall I not take them as an earnest of the better to follow? How else can I regard them? For never, in the midst of good things of this lovely world, have I felt quite at home in it. Never has it shown me things lovely or grand enough to satisfy me. It is not all I should like for a place to live in. It may be that my unsatisfaction comes from not having eyes open enough, or keen enough, to see and understand what he has given; but it matters little whether the cause lie in the world or in myself, both being incomplete: God is, and all is well.

All that is needed to set the world right enough for me—and no empyrean heaven could be right for me without it—is, that I care for God as he cares for me; that my will and desires keep time and harmony with his music; that I have no thought that springs from myself apart from him; that my individuality have the freedom that belongs to it as born of his individuality, and be in no slavery to my body, or my ancestry, or my prejudices, or any impulse whatever from region unknown; that I be free by obedience to the law of my being, the live and live-making will by which life is life, and my life is myself.

George MacDonald (1824–1905), Scottish novelist and poet, was a Congregational minister but left the pastorate in 1853 to devote himself to writing. His novels were largely based on life in the northeast of Scotland. His books reveal a firm and optimistic Christian faith and moral enthusiasm. MacDonald's abundant writings were an influence on C. S. Lewis, and much of his fiction has been republished in an updated format during the past two decades.

CHAPTER 3

Longing for Heaven

Drawn to Heaven

JOHANN MATTHÄUS MEYFART—1626

Jerusalem, whose towers touch the skies,
  I yearn to come to you!
Your shining streets have drawn my longing eyes
  My lifelong journey through.
And though I roam the woodland,
  The city, and the plain,
My heart still seeks the good land,
  My Father's house to gain.

O happy day, O blessed, happy hour,
  When will you come at last?
When fearless to my Father's loving pow'r,
  Whose word continues fast,
My soul I gladly render,
  For surely will this hand
Lead me with guidance tender
  To heaven's promised land.

Saints robed in white before the shining throne
  Their joyful anthems raise,
Till heaven's arches echo with the tone
  Of that great hymn of praise,

And all its host rejoices,
    And all its blessed throng
Unite their myriad voices
    In one eternal song.

JOHANN MATTHÄUS MEYFART (1590–1642) was a German minister and educator concerned with reforming the practices of both church and school. Against the worldliness of his time, he sought to redirect Christians toward their heavenly destiny, though he saw no contradiction between the hope of heaven and the successful pursuit of one's earthly vocation.

Hope in the Face of Death

JOHN BAILLIE—1933

THERE HAS BEEN in the Christian religion all through its history as deep a tragic sense as has ever appeared in the world. It has always given death a vitally important place in its scheme, refusing to regard it as a thing of secondary consequence, whether as a natural ending or as a mere milestone on a longer journey—or "a door to another room." Rather has it insisted on death as a most solemn crisis and extremity, a threshold of eternal judgment, on the brink of which we are all at every moment standing! . . .

And yet it is not by this note of crisis and tragedy that the Christian spirit has ever allowed itself to be finally dominated but by the note, precisely, of joy and good cheer. To it the ultimate fact is not death but life, not the Cross but the Resurrection and the Crown. It is what it is only because it is persuaded that the sting of death has been drawn and the grave robbed of its victory; so that death has no more dominion over us. It is frankly recognised that in its own self-enclosed and untransfigured nature, as it must present itself to those who do not share any such persuasion, death must be a ghastly and terrible thing; and indeed it is thus that death always *has* presented itself to sincere and profound unbelief. To see one's beloved stamped into the sod for his body to rot and the worms to eat him . . . and then to be of good cheer! No, there can be no good cheer unless it be true that that to which this dreadful thing has happened is not really one's beloved *himself* but only his earthly tabernacle; unless it be true that "the world passeth away, and the lust thereof: but he that doeth the will of God abideth for ever" (1 John 2:17 KJV). Whereas, therefore, it would be nothing but shallowness of spirit for one who had no hope beyond the grave to cease to be obsessed by the fact of death (whether by facing it cheerfully or by refusing to make it the object of his too constant thought), such a result in the soul of a Christian must rather be the mark of a great depth and maturity.

For biographical information on this author, see page 7.

I Would Not Live Always Below!

WILLIAM AUGUSTUS MUHLENBERG—MID-NINETEENTH CENTURY

I would not live alway—live alway below!
Oh no, I'll not linger when bidden to go:
The days of our pilgrimage granted us here
Are enough for life's woes, full enough for its cheer:
Would I shrink from the path which the prophets of God,
Apostles, and martyrs, so joyfully trod?
Like a spirit unblest, o'er the earth would I roam,
While brethren and friends are all hastening home?

I would not live alway: I ask not to stay
Where storm after storm rises dark o'er the way;
Where seeking for rest we but hover around,
Like the patriarch's bird, and no resting is found;
Where Hope, when she paints her gay bow in the air,
Leaves its brilliance to fade in the night of despair,
And joy's fleeting angel ne'er sheds a glad ray,
Save the gleam of the plumage that bears him away.

Chapter 3

I would not live alway—thus fettered by sin,
Temptation without and corruption within;
In a moment of strength if I sever the chain,
Scarce the victory's mine, ere I'm captive again;
E'en the rapture of pardon is mingled with fears,
And the cup of thanksgiving with penitent tears:
The festival trump calls for jubilant songs,
But my spirit her own *miserere* prolongs.

I would not live alway—no, welcome the tomb,
Since Jesus hath lain there I dread not its gloom;
Where he deigned to sleep, I'll too bow my head,
All peaceful to slumber on that hallowed bed.
Then the glorious daybreak, to follow that night,
The orient gleam of the angels of light,
With their clarion call for the sleepers to rise
And chant forth their matins, away to the skies.

Who, who would live alway? away from his God,
Away from yon heaven, that blissful abode,
Where the rivers of pleasure flow o'er the bright plains,
And the noontide of glory eternally reigns;
Where the saints of all ages in harmony meet,
Their Saviour and brethren transported to greet,
While the songs of salvation exultingly roll
And the smile of the Lord is the feast of the soul.

That heavenly music! what is it I hear?
The notes of the harpers ring sweet in mine ear!
And see, soft unfolding those portals of gold,
The King all arrayed in his beauty behold!
Oh give me, oh give me, the wings of a dove,
To adore him—be near him—enwrapt with his love;
I but wait for the summons, I list for the word—
Alleluia—Amen—evermore with the Lord!

WILLIAM AUGUSTUS MUHLENBERG (1796–1877) was an American clergyman, poet, and philanthropist. He was a great-grandson of American Lutheran pioneer Heinrich Melchior Mühlenberg, but left the Lutheran communion for the Episcopal Church and eventually became rector of the Church of the Holy Communion in New York City. In addition to his clerical duties and literary activity, he was co-founder and first superintendent of St. Luke's Hospital and was influential in promoting the unity of evangelical bodies throughout the world.

The Taste of Heaven

DAVID HANEY—1999

MY FAVORITE RESTAURANT in America is located here in Dallas. It is a wonderful place called Star Canyon, and it features a creative Southwestern cuisine. The most famous item on their unusual menu is a specially prepared rib eye steak. Anyone who goes to Star Canyon should be required by law to eat it at least once. Yet this is not the most unique feature of this wonderful restaurant. For at Star Canyon, each menu features a full page of delightfully exotic appetizers—a full 50 percent of the menu.

One of the first times I was there, I had a marvelous shrimp fajita appetizer unlike anything I had ever tasted in my life. I discovered taste buds that I did not even know I had. I could not believe that anyone could make something so odd-sounding taste so good.

When our waiter returned to inquire how our appetizers were, I informed him that I would not be needing anything else for the rest of the meal. The shrimp fajita had done me in. I was not planning to brush my teeth for the next week so that the flavor of that marvelous appetizer might linger in my mouth.

After the waiter had politely finished with his professional chuckling, he said, "If you thought that was good, just wait for the rib eye." My eyes lit up like a child who had just seen his name on the biggest present under the Christmas tree. How could anything be better? Was he serious, or was that just waiter-speak? My anticipation was on overload as I waited for the tantalizing rib eye.

Consider the implications: If this rib eye steak was better than what I had already tasted, it would be the best thing I had ever eaten in my life. . . . I had tasted the heavenly appetizer, and now I was groaning with each passing moment, waiting for the arrival of the heavenly main course. . . .

I have not forgotten the lesson of the appetizer. On its own, it was amazing. It was a meal all by itself. But it was not the main course; it was simply the foretaste. If I thought the appetizer was great, the rest of the meal was even more spectacular.

In some way this is why the suffering makes sense—because this life is not the entrée. Being satisfied with the appetizer makes as much sense as being satisfied with just being pregnant. Part of our struggle is that we know this is not all there is. We have tasted heaven, and yet we ache for more. If even the creation groans for a day of redemption, then should we expect any less discomfort? This life was never meant to "fill us up"; it is only created to prepare us for the "main course."

We live in a world of moral and spiritual pollution, and we long for the clear air of heaven. But this longing is not pointless, for we anticipate, along with all of creation, a place and time when we will no longer struggle but will receive our full adoption as children.

All of our suffering is mingled with our dissatisfaction in this life and anticipation of heaven. We should not be surprised at our struggle, for we not only live in a fallen and mutinous world, but we have already received the firstfruits of our deliverance. Of course we ache! We are groaning for the entrée, for the delivery, for the fulfillment of heaven. . . .

This promise of a hope still future sustains us through the injustices and inexplicable trials of this life. It is the hope of heaven.

Along with faith and love, hope forms the third fundamental pillar of the Christian life. Hope is as important to the believer as both love and faith, and it is just as deep. . . . Christians in the midst of the trials of life can endure only if they will focus clearly on the day when all things will be made new, made known, and made right. This promise of a hope still future sustains us through the injustices and inexplicable trials of this life. It is the hope of heaven. . . .

Why on earth must we wait patiently for the time when our hope will become sight? . . . How are we to be patient when what we await is the most desirable thing we could ever imagine? . . .

I suppose that most middle class Americans of the Baby Boomer generation share my memories of Christmas, or more precisely, the memories of the hours before Christmas morning. These were some of the longest hours in my life. . . . In all of my childhood experience, I never knew such anticipation. . . .

Isn't this the attitude we should have toward heaven?

If the glory of eternity, the presence of Christ, and the reunion of the saints are not our most anticipated moments, then what are?

Is not our discomfort with the wait an expression of our longing and our hope?

Shouldn't we be scratching and clawing at the gates of heaven, anxious for them to open?

DAVID HANEY is senior pastor of Riverbend Church in Austin, Texas. He attained degrees from Philadelphia College of the Bible, Dallas Theological Seminary, and Biola University, and regularly speaks across the country and around the world.

Heaven I Cannot Lose

EDNA DEAN PROCTOR— *circa* 1870

Now Summer finds her perfect prime;
        Sweet blows the wind from western calms;
On every bower red roses climb;
        The meadows sleep in mingled balms.
Nor stream, nor bank the wayside by,
        But lilies float and daisies throng;

Nor space of blue and sunny sky
That is not cleft with soaring song.
O flowery morns, O tuneful eves,
Fly swift! my soul ye cannot fill!
Bring the ripe fruit, the garnered sheaves,
The drifting snows on plain and hill.
Alike, to me, fall frosts and dews;
But Heaven, O Lord, I cannot lose!

Warm hands to-day are clasped in mine;
Fond hearts my mirth or mourning share;
And, over hope's horizon line,
The future dawns, serenely fair.
Yet still, though fervent vow denies,
I know the rapture will not stay;
Some wind of grief or doubt will rise
And turn my rosy sky to gray.
I shall awake, in rainy morn,
To find my hearth left lone and drear;
Thus, half in sadness, half in scorn,
I let my life burn on as clear
Though friends grow cold or fond love woos;
But Heaven, O Lord, I cannot lose!

In golden hours the angel Peace
Comes down and broods me with her wings:
I gain from sorrow sweet release;
I mate me with divinest things;
When shapes of guilt and gloom arise
And far the radiant angel flees,
My song is lost in mournful sighs,
My wine of triumph left but lees;
In vain for me her pinions shine,
And pure, celestial days begin;
Earth's passion-flowers I still must twine,
Nor braid one beauteous lily in

Ah! is it good or ill I choose?
But Heaven, O Lord, I cannot lose!

So wait I. Every day that dies
    With flush and fragrance born of June,
I know shall more resplendent rise
    Where summer needs nor sun nor moon.
And every bud, on love's low tree,
    Whose mocking crimson flames and falls,
In fullest flower I yet shall see
    High- blooming by the jasper walls.
Nay, every sin that dims my days,
    And wild regrets that veil the sun,
Shall fade before those dazzling rays,
    And my long glory be begun!
Let the years come to bless or bruise:
Thy Heaven, O Lord, I shall not lose!

EDNA DEAN PROCTOR (1829–1923) was born in Henniker, New Hampshire, where a bridge is named after her. She became a teacher in Woodstock, Connecticut, and later a governess in Brooklyn, New York. Her first book of poetry was published in 1867. Her poem "Heaven, O Lord, I Cannot Lose" was reprinted in several nineteenth-century anthologies. She also wrote on foreign travel and edited the sermons of the famous Brooklyn preacher Henry Ward Beecher. She died in Framingham, Massachusetts.

Heavenly Revelation

JOE BEAM—2000

SOMETIMES I THINK ABOUT what it will be like when I stumble through heaven, overwhelmed at all that is around me, swiveling my head rapidly to take it all in. I'll see angels of all kinds, godly people singing, and the Loving Light streaming from the throne.

Somewhere, sometime in that introduction to the home of God, I expect to hear an angel call my name. He'll know me, though I won't yet know him.

"Joe, Good to see you here. Welcome home."

"Thank you, I'm glad I'm here. I . . . I . . . I don't know what to say or what to ask. I'm reeling, staggered by the splendor."

"Take your time. Worship the King. You'll be here forever; there's no need to be in any hurry about anything."

"Wait. Before you leave, may I ask one thing? You know me. How? Do you angels know everything?"

"No. There is much we don't know. I know you because we've met before—at least in a manner of speaking. I was there, watching, helping, guarding. You just didn't know I was there."

"When? Can you tell me when and what was happening? I've wanted to know these things for a long time. Make them clear for me. Tell me what happened."

"Well, I wasn't always the angel sent to help you. But I remember once when . . ."

And so I expect it to go. I won't worship him, but I'll surely thank him. And all the others.

So will you.

Joe Beam has served as minister for growing churches in Georgia, Indiana, and Alabama. He is the founder and chairman of the board of Family Dynamics Institute, a nonprofit organization that uses the latest scientific and most creative methods to strengthen families. Before founding Family Dynamics, Joe served as president of Change Dynamics International, a successful resource development and training company. Since 1970, Joe has spoken to more than two million people worldwide.

I Don't Know When

EMILY DICKINSON— *circa* 1859

Going to Heaven!
I don't know when—
Pray do not ask me how!
Indeed I'm too astonished
To think of answering you!
Going to Heaven!
How dim it sounds!
And yet it will be done
As sure as flocks go home at night
Unto the Shepherd's arm!

Perhaps you're going too!
Who knows?
If you should get there first
Save just a little place for me
Close to the two I lost—
The smallest "Robe" will fit me
And just a bit of "Crown"—
For you know we do not mind our dress
When we are going home—

I'm glad I don't believe it
For it would stop my breath—
And I 'd like to look a little more
At such a curious Earth!
I am glad they did believe it
Whom I have never found
Since the mighty Autumn afternoon
I left them in the ground.

For biographical information on this author, see page 11.

Chapter 3

Oz

Calvin Miller—1996

Growing up in a part of Oklahoma which is very close to Kansas, I have often thought of Oz. In fact, I once went to southwest Kansas to show the children where *The Wizard of Oz* was written. Kansas is of the earth, and Kansans are busy people who live in Kansas and think about Kansas a lot. I once thought a lot about Kansas. But now I am older. Kansas intrigues me less and less. Now I think more of Oz than of Kansas. . . .

Hebrews 12:1–2 seems to discuss those saints in heaven who look down on earth:

> *Therefore, since we are surrounded by such a great cloud of witnesses, let us throw off everything that hinders and the sin that so easily entangles, and let us run with perseverance the race marked out for us. Let us fix our eyes on Jesus, the author and perfecter of our faith, who for the joy set before him endured the cross, scorning its shame, and sat down at the right hand of the throne of God.*

It is easier to live in Oz, says Hebrews, and look for Kansas, than to live in Kansas and search for Oz. In Kansas, everybody has a theory about Oz. Streets of gold it has—they say. A crystal sea, too. There is a throne with lightning. The all powerful one forbids evil and crushes witches while munchkins dance on yellow brick roads.

I've ministered to hundreds of dying people across my thirty-five years as a pastor. I've stood at many black-draped lecterns and told the grieving all I knew of Oz. Once I waited with a dying friend and heard him say, "I'm crossing over, pastor. Be here as I cross." He crossed and closed his eyes and opened them in the world I so much wanted to know about. "Tell me . . . what's it like?" I wanted to say, but he left me on the bank and stepped into the mist. Like Arthur, enshrouded in fog, he left me, and Oz remained a mystery. . . .

Here and there some may return from Oz. In John 12 is the curious case of Martha of Bethany giving a dinner for Jesus. It was the least she could do for the man who had just raised her brother from the dead. But John says that a great many people had come out from Jerusalem (see John 12:9) to see Lazarus who would, of course, have been there eating. There is something quite believable about this story. It is most curious to watch a formerly dead man eat. Many of these who had earlier come to his funeral were now watching him do just that.

Could Lazarus have been the celebrity that all but eclipsed the glory of his great Redeemer? Well, he was back from Oz and his return was the subject of much conversation. In John 11:35 when Jesus brought him back from the grave, he wept. There are as many speculations given to Jesus' tears as there are theologians. But Jesus may very well have wept because he felt grief in calling Lazarus back from the Emerald City. . . .

We cannot help but wonder if Jesus wept in Bethany because he knew the truth. The city from which he recalled Lazarus was so much better than the harsh Bethany where his sisters wished him to be. Bethany, where the harshness of life would, for Lazarus, at last culminate in his second funeral. Jesus wept (John 11:35). Of course, he did. It's a crying matter to take some one from Oz and plop them down in stormy Kansas.

And we cannot help but wonder about the fictional Dorothy, as she lived out her years in rural Kansas. Long after Toto was in the pet cemetery outside Dodge City, where was Dorothy? Did she not yearn for that long-lost land of song and citadels? Jesus made it clear: Once you've caught a glimpse of Oz, Kansas is never quite good enough again.

CALVIN MILLER, pastor, author, and seminary professor has written more than forty books. He is currently on the faculty of Samford University's Beeson Divinity School in Birmingham, Alabama.

Chapter 3

A Softer Paradise

SHIRLEY ANNE LEONARD—2002

Gold is hard and cold
and diamonds glitter
with indifferent light.

Silver shines with glacial
overtones, gems are
beautiful but unimpressed
by tears at night.

Give me a living rose
intimate with dew,
and gardens rich with life,
sparkling waterfalls
and sleek birds soaring
over trees—
a loving hand to hold
by a living stream,
with Paradise restored
in Eden moonlight.

SHIRLEY ANNE LEONARD is a poetess and writer residing in Hamilton and Wheaton, Illinois. Her verse grows out of both a hunger for God and some difficult life experiences, including widowhood after caring for a husband during his long illness. She is mother of five and grandmother of eight, and is married to Richard Leonard, a compiler of this volume.

The Hope of Heaven

CORRIE TEN BOOM WITH JOHN AND ELIZABETH SHERRILL—1971

I REACHED THE WINDOW and cupped my eyes to peer in. A nurse was standing directly between me and Betsie. I ducked out of sight, waited a minute, then looked again. A second nurse had joined the first, both now standing where I wanted to see. They stepped to the head and foot of the bed: I gazed curiously at what lay on it. It was a carving in old yellow ivory. There was no clothing on the figure; I could see each ivory rib, and the outline of the teeth through the parchment cheeks.

It took me a moment to realize it was Betsie.

The nurses had each seized two corners of the sheet. They lifted it between them and carried the bundle from the room before my heart had started to beat again in my chest.

Betsie! But—she had too much to do! She could not—

Where were they taking her? Where had they gone! I turned from the window and began running along the side of the building, chest hurting me as I breathed.

Then I remembered the washroom. That window at the rear—that was where . . .

My feet carried me mechanically around to the back of the building. And there, with my hand on the windowsill, I stopped. Suppose she was there? Suppose they had laid Betsie on that floor?

I started walking again. I walked for a long time, still with that pain in my chest. And each time my feet took me back to the washroom window. I would not go in. I would not look. Betsie could not be there. . . .

"Corrie!"

I turned around to see Mien running after me. "Corrie, I've looked for you everywhere! Oh, Corrie, come!"

She seized my arm and drew me toward the back of the hospital.

When I saw where she was headed I wrenched my arm free. "I know, Mien. I know already."

She didn't seem to hear. She seized me again, led me to the washroom window, and pushed me in ahead of her. In the reeking room stood a nurse. I drew back in alarm, but Mien was behind me.

"This is the sister," Mien said to the nurse.

I turned my head to the side—I would not look at the bodies that lined the far wall. Mien put an arm around my shoulder and drew me across the room till we were standing above that heart-breaking row.

"Corrie! Do you see her!"

I raised my eyes to Betsie's face. Lord Jesus—what have You done! Oh Lord, what are You saying! What are You giving me!

For there lay Betsie, her eyes closed as if in sleep, her face full and young. The care lines, the grief lines, the deep hollows of hunger and disease were simply gone. In front of me was the Betsie of Haarlem, happy and at peace. Stronger! Freer! This was the Betsie of heaven bursting with joy and health. Even her hair was graciously in place as if an angel had ministered to her.

At last I turned wonderingly to Mien. The nurse went silently to the door and opened it for us herself. "You can leave through the hall," she said softly.

I looked once more at the radiant face of my sister. Then Mien and I left the room together. A pile of clothes was heaped outside in the hallway; on top lay Nollie's blue sweater.

I stooped to pick it up. The sweater is threadbare and stained with newsprint, but it was a tangible link with Betsie. Mien seized my arm. "Don't touch those things! Black lice! They'll all be burned."

And so I left behind the last physical tie. It was just as well. It was better. Now what tied me to Betsie was the hope of heaven.

Corrie ten Boom (1892–1983), born in the Netherlands, was imprisoned by the Nazis during World War II after her family had sheltered several Jewish families. She survived the dreaded Ravensbruck concentration camp and then traveled ceaselessly, carrying her message of triumphant living around the world. A colorful, amusing speaker, she also authored several books, the best known being *The Hiding Place.*

Longing for Departed Friends

HENRY VAUGHAN — 1650

They are all gone into the world of light!
    And I alone sit lingring here!
Their very memory is fair and bright,
    And my sad thoughts doth clear.

It glows and glitters in my cloudy brest
    Like stars upon some gloomy grove,
Or those faint beams in which this hill is drest
    After the Sun's remove.

I see them walking in an air of glory,
    Whose light doth trample on my days:
My days, which are at best but dull and hoary,
    Meer glimmering and decays.

O holy Hope! and high Humility!
    High as the heavens above;
These are your walks, and you have shew'd them me
    To kindle my cold love.

Dear, beauteous death; the Jewel of the Just!
    Shining no where, but in the dark;
What mysteries do lie beyond thy dust,
    Could man outlook that mark!

He that hath found some fledg'd bird's nest may know
    At first sight if the bird be flown;
But what fair well or grove he sings in now,
    That is to him unknown.

And yet, as Angels in some brighter dreams
    Call to the soul when man doth sleep,

So some strange thoughts transcend our wonted theams,
    And into glory peep.

If a star were confin'd into a tomb,
    Her captive flames must needs burn there;
But when the hand that lockt her up gives room,
    She'll shine through all the sphere.

O Father of eternal life, and all
    Created glories under thee!
Resume thy spirit from this world of thrall
    Into true liberty!

Either disperse these mists, which blot and fill
    My perspective still as they pass;
Or else remove me hence unto that hill,
    Where I shall need no glass.

HENRY VAUGHAN (1622–1695) studied medicine and entered into a career as a physician. After experiencing a spiritual transformation, he began to publish poetry marked by an intense and sustained spiritual fervor. Though his work fell into neglect in his time, he came to be numbered with the British "metaphysical poets," such as John Donne, and exercised an influence on later writers, such as Wordsworth.

Crossing the Bar

ALFRED TENNYSON—1889

Sunset and evening star,
    And one clear call for me!
And may there be no moaning of the bar,
    When I put out to sea,

But such a tide as moving seems asleep,
    Too full for sound and foam.
When that which drew from out the boundless deep
    Turns again home.

Twilight and evening bell,
    And after that the dark!
And may there be no sadness of farewell,
    When I embark;

For tho' from out our bourne of Time and Place
    The flood may bear me far,
I hope to see my Pilot face to face
    When I have crost the bar.

For biographical information on this author, see page 6.

CHAPTER 4

At Home in Heaven

A Place Prepared

Eliza E. Hewitt—1898

Sing the wondrous love of Jesus,
   Sing His mercy and His grace;
In the mansions bright and blessed
   He'll prepare for us a place.

While we walk the pilgrim pathway
   Clouds will overspread the sky;
But when trav'ling days are over,
   Not a shadow, not a sigh.

Let us then be true and faithful,
   Trusting, serving every day;
Just one glimpse of Him in glory
   Will the toils of life repay.

Onward to the prize before us!
   Soon His beauty we'll behold;
Soon the pearly gates will open,
   We shall tread the streets of gold.

When we all get to heaven,
   What a day of rejoicing that will be!

When we all see Jesus,
We'll sing and shout the victory.

Eliza Edmunds Hewitt (1851–1920), of Philadelphia, was an active Sunday-school worker and writer, although a spinal problem left her an invalid for most of her life.

A Homing Instinct

Peter Kreeft—1980

Let's explore our blessing. Let's open our strange present and play with it a bit. What does it mean?

Alienation is the opposite of being at home. If the Bible is not wrong when it calls us "strangers and pilgrims" (1 Peter 2:11 KJV), then that's why we feel alienation: We feel what *is*. When any organism is at home, there is an ecological fit with its environment, a harmony, a rightness. If the environment does not supply this, that environment is not its home.

A fish has no quarrel with the sea. Yet we have a lover's quarrel with the world. . . .

We have a homing instinct, a "home detector," and it doesn't ring for earth. That's why nearly every society in history except our own instinctively believes in life after death. Like the great mythic wanderers, like Ulysses and Aeneas, we have been trying to get home. Earth just doesn't smell like home. However good a road it is, however good a motel it is, however good a training camp it is, it is not home. Heaven is.

Heaven means not just a pleasant place but our place, not just a good place but a good place for us.

Play with that thought for a minute: Heaven is *home*. Experiment with the thought; feel the gem; look at the picture; explore the house before deciding whether to buy. Heaven means not just a pleasant place but *our* place, not just a good place but a good place for us. We fit there.

PETER KREEFT is professor of philosopy at Boston College and the author of more than forty-five books. He is a regular contributor to several Christian publications and is in wide demand as a speaker at conferences.

The Blessed Homeland

FANNY J. CROSBY—1877

Gliding o'er life's fitful waters,
Heavy surges sometimes roll;
And we sigh for yonder haven,
For the Homeland of the soul.

Oft we catch a faint reflection
Of its bright and vernal hills;
And, tho' distant, how we hail it!
How each heart with rapture thrills!

To our Father, and our Saviour,
To the Spirit, Three in One,
We shall sing glad songs of triumph
When our harvest work is done.

'Tis the weary pilgrim's Homeland,
Where each throbbing care shall cease,
And our longings and our yearnings,
Like a wave, be hushed to peace.

Refrain:

Blessed Homeland, ever fair!
Sin can never enter there;

But the soul, to life awaking,
Everlasting bloom shall wear.

Frances Jane Van Alstyne (1820–1915), known by her maiden name as Fanny J. Crosby, lost her sight at the age of six weeks. She became a pupil, then a teacher, at the New York City Institution for the Blind, and began writing poetry at an early age. In 1858 she married the blind musician Alexander Van Alstyne. Beginning in 1864, Fanny Crosby published more than two thousand hymns, many of them under other names because music publishers were embarrassed by the quantity of her output. Although she is not judged an outstanding poet, the simplicity and earnestness of her verse has endeared her songs to Christian worshipers. Favorites today include "All the Way My Savior Leads Me," "Blessed Assurance," "Nearer the Cross," "Pass Me Not, O Gentle Savior," "Rescue the Perishing," and "To God Be the Glory."

An Appetite for Eternity

Sheldon Vanauken — 1977

If, indeed, we all have a kind of appetite for eternity, we have allowed ourselves to be caught up in a society that frustrates our longing at every turn. Half our inventions are advertised to save time—the washing machine, the fast car, the jet flight—but for what? Never were people more harried by time: by watches, by buzzers, by time clocks, by precise schedules, by the beginning of the programme. There is, in fact, *some* truth in "the good old days": no other civilisation of the past was ever so harried by time.

And yet, why not? Time is our natural environment. We live in time as we live in the air we breathe. And we love the air—who has not taken deep breaths of pure, fresh country air, just for the pleasure of it? How strange that we cannot love time. It spoils our loveliest moments. Nothing quite comes up to expectation because of it. We alone: animals, so far as we can see, are unaware of time, untroubled. Time *is* their natural environment. Why do we sense that it is not ours?

Chapter 4

We were created for eternity. Not only are we harried by time, we seem unable, despite a thousand generations, even to get used to it.

C. S. Lewis, in his second letter to me at Oxford, asked how it was that I, as a product of a materialistic universe, was not at home there. "Do fish complain of the sea for being wet? Or if they did, would that fact itself not strongly suggest that they had not always been, or wd. not always be, purely aquatic creatures?" Then, if we complain of time and take such joy in the seemingly timeless moment, what does that suggest?

It suggests that we have not always been or will not always be purely temporal creatures. It suggests that we were created for eternity. Not only are we harried by time, we seem unable, despite a thousand generations, even to get used to it. We are always amazed at it—how fast it goes, how slowly it goes, how much of it is gone. Where, we cry, has the time gone? We aren't adapted to it, not at home in it. If that is so, it may appear as a proof, or at least a powerful suggestion, that eternity exists and is our home.

So it appeared to me. It appeared to me that Davy and I had longed for timelessness—eternity—all our days; and the longing coupled with my post-mortem vision of the total Davy whetted my appetite for heaven. Golden streets and compulsory harp lessons may lack appeal—but timelessness? And total persons? Heaven is, indeed, *home.*

Sheldon Vanauken (1914–1996) was a sharp young literature student in Virginia and an agnostic when he became fascinated by C. S. Lewis and Oxford's Christian tradition. The two men exchanged letters and eventually became friends. Lewis was elated when Vanauken became a Christian and went on to become an author. His best-known work, *A Severe Mercy,* relates how he and his wife, Jean (called Davy), faced her impending death.

My Home Is Yonder

FROM *LYRA GERMANICA*
TRANSLATED BY CATHERINE WINKWORTH—1858

A pilgrim here I wander,
On earth have no abode;
My fatherland is yonder,
My home is with my God.
For here I journey to and fro,
There, in eternal rest,
Will God His gracious gift bestow
On all the toil-oppressed.

For what hath life been giving
From youth up till this day,
But constant toil and striving,
Far back as thought can stray?
How many a day of toil and care,
How many a night of tears,
Hath pass'd in grief that none could share,
In lonely anxious fears!

How many a storm hath lighten'd
And thundered round my path!
And winds and rains have frighten'd
My heart with fiercest wrath;
And cruel envy, hatred, scorn,
Have darken'd oft my lot;
And patiently reproach I've borne,
Though I deserved it not.

Then through this life of dangers
I'll onward take my way,
For in this land of strangers
I do not think to stay.

Still forward on the road I fare
    That leads me to my home.
My Father's comfort waits me there,
    When I have overcome.

Ah, yes! my home is yonder,
    Where all the angelic bands
Praise Him with awe and wonder,
    In whose Almighty hands
All things that are and shall be, lie,
    By Him upholden still,
Who casteth down and lifts on high
    At His most holy will

That home have I desired;
    'Tis there I would be gone;
Till I am well nigh tir'd,
    O'er earth I've journey'd on;
The longer here I roam, I find
    The less of real joy
That e'er could please or fill my mind,
    For all hath some alloy.

Where now my spirit stayeth
    It is not her true abode;
This earthly house decayeth,
    And she will drop its load.
When comes the hour to leave beneath
    What now I use and have,
And when I've yielded up my breath,
    Earth gives me but a grave.

But Thou, my joy and gladness,
    Jesus, my life and light,
Wilt raise me from this sadness,
    This long tempestuous night,

Into the perfect gladsome day,
  Where, bathed in joy divine,
Among Thy saints, and bright as they,
  I too shall ever shine.

There shall I dwell for ever,
  Not as a guest alone,
With those who cease there never
  To worship at Thy throne;
There in my heritage I'll rest,
  From baser things set free,
And join the chorus of the blest
  For ever, Lord, to Thee!

THIS HYMN is found in *Lyra Germanica,* a collection of German hymns translated into English by CATHERINE WINKWORTH (1827–1878), of Manchester, England. She was the foremost nineteenth-century translator of German hymns into English. Her translations, still found in many hymnals, include "Now Thank We All Our God" and "Praise to the Lord, the Almighty."

Drawn Home to Heaven

E. M. BOUNDS—1921

THE CHRISTIAN'S ATTITUDE is toward heaven, not to die, merely to be unclothed of the present. It is not simply to get rid of the cumbrance of the tent-like bodies. It is not death, for death has no charms for the true Christian. He fears not to die, he fears not to live. Life has for him little charms apart from heaven. Death has no charms aside from heaven.

The attitude is thus given by Paul: "For we that are in this tabernacle do groan, being burdened; not for that we would be unclothed, but clothed upon, that mortality might be swallowed up of life." This supposes a desire so full of light, of expectations, of longings, that it burdens. Heaven is so charmful to the unclouded vision of faith, so bright and deathless under the rosy hues of an immortal hope, that the present burdens become an intolerable load. To stay is to live in the graveyard, to have a home in a decaying house, to be dying. Earth is a vast cemetery. Everything betokens death, breathes death and is dying. The desire of heaven is kindled at the fountain of life where we become sick of the dead and sick of the dying. The soul, having tasted of the spring of life, longs to bathe in its full river, and yearns to plunge in its immeasurable ocean.

Materialized times always make much of earth and little of heaven. True religion always makes little of earth and much of heaven.

The attitude for heaven is the desire of life for life, of life against death. Here death reigns, imprisons and ruins. There life reigns, emancipates and enriches. We are impatiently patient for life eternal, life which is found nowhere else but in heaven. Sick of death, we aspire to life by living and longing for heaven. This groaning for heaven is not natural. Nature is of the earth, earthly. The Holy Spirit changes nature and fashions us for heaven. "Now he that hath wrought us for the selfsame thing is God, who also hath given us the earnest of the Spirit" (2 Corinthians 5:5 KJV).

God has fashioned us for this heavenly life. He implants in us these heavenly desires. When we stand thus attested to heaven, thus looking toward heaven, thus longing for heaven, these are the marks of God's hand, the results of His work of grace in our hearts. He puts in us the Holy Spirit to keep the memory freighted with and alive to the fact of heaven, to keep the desires ardent for heaven, to keep the hands busy for heaven and to keep the taste sweet and fresh for heaven. God works this mighty heavenly work in us so that we look not at the things which are temporal, value not the things which are insipid and transitory, and strive not after the perishing things of earth.

These are materialized and materializing times. Materialized times always make much of earth and little of heaven. True religion always makes little of earth and much of heaven. If God's watchmen are not brave, Argus-eyed, and sleepless, religion will catch the contagion of the times, and think little of and struggle less for heaven.

God makes much of heaven. He was the architect and builder of its magnificence and glory. It is His dwelling place, His city, by preeminence, His capital, His metropolis, the home of His family, the dwelling place of His earthly elect. God fashions every child of His after the pattern of heaven, feeds every child of His on its food, trains every soldier of His for its warfare, and begets in every child of His insatiable thirstings for heaven. When the taste is dull heavenward and the eye dim heavenward, then the luster of God has faded from the spirit, the work of God is checked in the soul, the life of God pulsates feebly, and the love of God is chilled to the heart.

"For the selfsame thing"—this heavenly fashion, these heavenly tastes and heavenly longings—says the apostle, has God "wrought us" and "given us the earnest of his Spirit." Not only does this work of God wrought in us shape and mold us after the heavenly, but the true work of God in us gives a foretaste and pledge of the heavenly.

To the true Christian, heaven is not a mere sentiment, or poetry, or dreamland, but real solid and abiding granite in strength, home-drawing in sweetness and influence. God is never happier, never better to His earthly saints than when their heavenly trend is strongly marked. Heavenly longings and heavenly goings are plainly and emphatically declared of the saints whose devotion to heaven has unloosed and estranged them from earth. He is not ashamed to be called their God. For them He hath prepared a city. What does God think of us who have no sighings for heaven, no longings for it; earth, earthly, earthened? God's throne is in heaven. His power, person and glory are preeminently there. Does God attract and hold us? Then heaven attracts and holds. . . .

Heaven ought to draw and engage us. Heaven ought to so fill our hearts and hands, our manner and our conversation, our character and our features, that all would see that we are foreigners, strangers to this world, natives of a nobler clime, fairer than this. Out of tune, out of harmony, out of course, we must be with this world. The very atmosphere of the world should be chilling to us and noxious, its suns eclipsed and its companionship dull and insipid. Heaven is our native land and home to us, and death to us is not the dying hour, but the birth hour. Heaven should kindle desire, and like a magnet draw us upward to the skies. Duty, inexorable duty, fealty to God, alone, should hold us here. . . .

At home in heaven! What welcome! What satisfaction! What rest to tired feet, and tired hearts! What a sense of security and confidence! The home feelings in full opulence of richest wealth! Nowhere on earth's green, glad soil will the home feeling be so profound, so satisfying, so restful, and so happifying as in heaven. It is not only to be realized as home when we get there, but all along the way the home feeling is to draw and bind us to that heavenly world. The homesickness for heaven is to alienate us from earth, make us sick at heart and beget pinings for home.

With deep spiritual insight and the soundest spiritual philosophy did one of Scotland's most gifted and saintly preachers say after visiting a beautiful Manse: "The Manse is altogether too sweet. Other men could hardly live there without saying, this is my rest. I don't think ministers' manses should ever be so beautiful."

This is not splenetic, nor overdrawn, but the assertion of a great principle to guard against a great peril. Great earthly attachments lessen heavenly attachments. The heart which indulges itself in great earthly loves will have less for heaven. God's great work and often His most afflictive and chastening work is to unfasten our hearts from earth and fasten them to heaven, to break up and desolate the earthly home that we may seek a home in heaven.

Edward McKendree Bounds (1835–1913) trained for the law, but instead served as a Methodist minister in Tennessee, Alabama, and St. Louis. During the Civil War he was a Confederate army chaplain. He spent his later years in Georgia working on devotional writings. Though few of his books were published during his lifetime, he later came to be recognized as a forceful and exemplary author on the subject of prayer. "Drawn to Heaven" was published posthumously in 1921.

Really Home

Randy Alcorn — 1996

SHE STARED AT THE COSMIC CENTER, intoxicated by his character. This was her only king. This her only kingdom. The character of God defined the landscape of heaven. The Carpenter had prepared a place all right. What a place!

Her family and old friends had greeted her. Finally she had a chance to ask her mother a question.

"Did he give you a special name too, Mama?"

"Yes. He gives one to all of his redeemed. Wherever you go you will be a testimony to one particular facet of his character, that reflected in your new name. Everyone who meets you will see something of Elyon they have never seen before."

Torel, the giant warrior who had carried her to this country, said, "It takes all the redeemed together to paint the picture of his character. Even then, the multitudes of his followers are insufficient. The caverns of the knowledge of God each lead to another and another and another. Should any explorer exhaust them on one world he can simply move to the next. There will always be more to learn, more to discover about him and his universe and his people. The learning will never cease, the reverence always deepen, the symphony of worship ever build, one crescendo upon another."

"But," Dani said, "I thought we would know everything here."

"A common error of Adam's race, one I can never comprehend," Torel said, looking puzzled. "Only Elyon knows everything. Creatures can never know everything. They are limited. They are learners. *We* are learners. You have already learned much here, have you not?"

"Yes," Dani said. "For one thing, I've learned why America never felt like home to me. For a time I'd thought maybe Africa was my home, but somehow I knew that wasn't right either. I always sensed I was on foreign ground. Whether it was in the city, the suburbs, the country, or on a tropical island, nothing there could be a permanent home. And given all the injustice and suffering, who would want it to be? I never fit in there, Torel. Sometimes I thought it was because of my skin color. Now I realize it was because of the God-shaped emptiness within me, the void that could only be filled by being in his presence. By being here."

Torel nodded, listening intently, as if he was not tutor but student.

"While on earth I kept hearing heaven's music," Dani said, "but it was elusive, more like an echo. All that clatter, all those competing sounds, all the television programs and ringing phones and traffic and voices drowned out Elyon's music. Sometimes I'd dance to the wrong beat, march to the wrong anthem. I was never made for that place. I was made for this one."

The wild rush of Joy, the rapture of discovery overwhelmed her as if she'd just gotten in on the greatest inside joke in the history of the universe. Now she saw and felt it with stunning clarity. Her unswerving patriotism had been reserved for another country. Every joy on earth, such as the joy of reunion, had been but an inkling, a whisper of greater Joy. Every place on earth had been at best a rented room, a place to spend the night on a long journey.

She remembered the rough sketches she used to make before starting to paint. "Mount Hood, Niagara Falls, the Grand Canyon, the Oregon Coast, all those places on earth were only rough sketches of this place. The best parts of the old world were sneak previews of this one. Like little foretastes, like licking the spoon from Mama's beef stew an hour before supper." She smiled at her mother and grabbed her hand.

"I'm home," she shouted, first hugging her mother, then grabbing the angel's hands and dancing in a circle, turning around and around and around, taking pleasure in his unfamiliarity and awkwardness at the dance, while her mother clapped a beat. "Did you hear me, Torel? I'm really home!"

For biographical information on this author, see page 34.

I Don't Belong (Sojourner's Song)

Gloria Gaither and Buddy Greene—1990

It's not home where men sell their souls
And the taste of power is sweet
Where wrong is right and neighbors fight
While the hungry are dying in the street
Where kids are abused and women are used
And the weak are crushed by the strong
Nations gone mad, Jesus is sad.
And I don't belong

I don't belong and I'm going someday
Home to my own native land

I don't belong and it seems like I hear
The sound of a welcome home band
I don't belong, well I'm a foreigner here
Just singing a sojourner's song
I've always known this place ain't home
And I don't belong

Gloria Gaither is well known not only as a songwriter and speaker, but also as a stateswoman of Christian ministry. Her impressive schedule includes creating songs, books, scripts, and formal papers, as well as lecturing.

Buddy Greene brings a wide variety of traditional influences to his music from country to gospel to blues. In addition to his reputation as a guitarist, songwriter, and singer, he is a world-class virtuoso harmonica player.

Chapter 4

Are We Home Yet?

Joseph M. Stowell—1995

Igniting the reality of heaven where I will be a real person in a real personalized place living with the reality of my risen Lord and Savior carries with it two profound revelations.

The first is that heaven is truly *home.* This realization gives rise to the second revelation: I am an *alien* and a *pilgrim* here. Saint John the Divine said it best, "God is at home; we are in the far country."

Webster's Ninth New Collegiate Dictionary notes that home is where our "domestic affections lie." As we used to say, "Home is where the heart is." That is why a cowboy can sing, "Home, home on the range" and why someone far away from his place of residence can exclaim, "I love this place; I feel so at home here." . . .

We, as heaven-bound pilgrims, are the real homeless ones on this planet. Christ never considered Himself at home here. He knew that He had come from heaven and that He was going back to heaven and that heaven was truly home. This left Him wonderfully unhindered in functioning on behalf of His Father's mission. The disciples had in a sense become homeless as well. They had given up their homes, careers, familiar places, and family to journey with Christ toward an eternal home.

The mission of Christ, as we have already noted, was never intended to culminate at the Cross. The Cross and the empty grave were merely a means to kick the door of heaven open for us so that we could go home to be with Him. Home is where you feel comfortable, secure, safe, and at peace.

I'm reminded of an elderly missionary couple who arrived at their home port after years of faithful service. At the dock, an ambassador and his wife who had returned on the ship with them were surrounded by a crowd. Roses were bestowed on his wife as photographers' flashes exploded, and an attentive, admiring press and public hung on every word as he spoke of the joy of serving his government and coming home. As the missionary couple walked unnoticed through the crowd, the wife, with hot tears streaking her face, wondered out loud to her husband, "Why is it that we have given our whole lives to Christ and yet there is no one here to honor us and welcome us home?" Her understanding husband, reaching beyond that lonely moment, said to her, "Honey, we're not home yet."

JOSEPH M. STOWELL holds degrees from Cedarville College, Dallas Theological Seminary, and Master's College. After serving as president of Moody Bible Institute for eighteen years, he now serves as teaching pastor of Harvest Bible Chapel in suburban Chicago. Joe is a frequent speaker at churches and conferences throughout the world. He is a prolific author.

Alone upon That Shore?

FREDERICK W. FABER—MID-NINETEENTH CENTURY

Alone! to land alone upon that shore.
With no one sight that we have ever seen before;
    Things of a different hue,
    And the sounds all new,
And fragrances so sweet the soul may faint.
Alone! Oh, that first hour of being a saint.

Alone! to land upon that shore,
On which no wavelets lisp, no billows roar,
    Perhaps no shape of ground,
    Perhaps no sight or sound,
No forms of earth our fancies to arrange—
But to begin, alone, that mighty change!

Alone! to land alone upon that shore,
Knowing so well we can return no more;
    No voice or face of friend,
    None with us to attend
Our disembarking on that awful strand,
But to arrive alone in such a land!

Alone! to land upon that shore!
To begin, alone to live forevermore,
　　To have no one to teach
　　The manners or the speech
Of that new life, or put us at our ease;
Oh! that we might die in pairs or companies!

Alone? The God we know is on that shore,
The God of whose attractions we know more
　　Than of those who may appear
　　Nearest and dearest here;
Oh, is He not the life-long friend we know
More privately than any friend below?

FREDERICK WILLIAM FABER (1814–1863), an Anglican clergyman, was ordained a Catholic priest in 1847 and became head of an oratory, or chapel, in London. Among his writings are many hymns, the best known of which is "Faith of Our Fathers."

A Deeper Country

C. S. LEWIS—1956

IT IS AS HARD TO EXPLAIN how this sunlit land was different from the old Narnia, as it would be to tell you how the fruits of that country taste. Perhaps you will get some idea of it, if you think like this. You may have been in a room in which there was a window that looked out on a lovely bay of the sea or a green valley that wound away among mountains. And in the wall of that room opposite to the window there may have been a looking glass. And as you turned away from the window you suddenly caught sight of that sea or that valley, all over again, in the looking glass. And the sea in the mirror, or the valley in the mirror, were in one sense just the same as the real ones; yet at the same time they were somehow different—deeper, more wonderful, more like places in a story: in a story you have never heard but very much want to know. The difference between the old Narnia and the new Narnia was like that. The new one was a deeper country; every rock and flower and blade of grass looked as if it meant more. I can't describe it any better than that; if you ever get there, you will know what I mean.

It was the Unicorn who summed up what everyone was feeling. He stamped his right forehoof on the ground and neighed and then cried,

"I have come home at last! This is my real country! I belong here. This is the land I have been looking for all my life, though I never knew it till now. The reason why we loved the old Narnia is that it sometimes looked a little like this. Bree-hee-hee! Come further up, come further in!" . . .

Then Aslan turned to them and said,

"You do not yet look so happy as I mean you to be."

Lucy said, "We're so afraid of being sent away, Aslan. And you have sent us back into our own world so often."

"No fear of that," said Aslan. "Have you not guessed?"

Their hearts leaped and a wild hope rose within them.

"There *was* a real railway accident," said Aslan softly. "Your father and mother and all of you are—as you used to call it in the Shadow-Lands—dead. The term is over: the holidays have begun. The dream is ended: this is the morning."

And as he spoke he no longer looked to them like a lion; but the things that began to happen after that were so great and beautiful that I cannot write them. And for us this is the end of all the stories, and we can most truly say that they all lived happily ever after. But for them it was only the beginning of the real story. All their life in this world and all their adventures in Narnia had only been the cover and the title page; now at last they were beginning Chapter One of the Great Story, which no one on earth has read; which goes on forever; in which every chapter is better than the one before.

For biographical information on this author, see page 10.

Chapter 4

Uphill All the Way

CHRISTINA GEORGINA ROSSETTI—1858

Does the road wind up-hill all the way?
    Yes, to the very end.
Will the day's journey take the whole long day?
    From morn to night, my friend.

But is there for the night a resting-place?
    A roof for when the slow, dark hours begin.
May not the darkness hide it from my face?
    You cannot miss that inn.

Shall I meet other wayfarers at night?
    Those who have gone before.
Then must I knock, or call when just in sight?
    They will not keep you standing at that door.

Shall I find comfort, travel-sore and weak?
    Of labour you shall find the sum.
Will there be beds for me and all who seek?
    Yea, beds for all who come.

For biographical information on this author, see page 13.

CHAPTER 5

Our Glory in Heaven

Heavenly Bodies

TIMOTHY GEORGE—2003

THE WORLD IN WHICH CHRISTIANITY arose affirmed the immortality of the soul, a cornerstone of Greek philosophy. Platonic arguments for the soul's innate immortality have influenced views about life after death from Gnosticism to the New Age movement today. The soul's immortality was a central tenet in Kant's philosophy and this was echoed in the triad of Protestant liberalism—the fatherhood of God, the brotherhood of man, and the immortality of the soul.

But biblical faith has always insisted on something very different. God's ultimate purpose for all his human creatures, for the lost as well as for the redeemed (see John 5:29, Acts 24:15), is not an eternal, incorporeal existence but rather the resurrection of the body. This concept has been offensive to human reason from the beginning, as Paul found out when he preached about Jesus and the Resurrection to the philosophers of Mars Hill (see Acts 17:22–34).

Yet belief in the bodily resurrection is so basic that it was included in the Apostles' Creed.

Why make such a fuss about the body? Because of three key moments in the history of salvation: Creation, Incarnation, and Redemption.

When God first created the material world, and human beings within it from the dust of the earth, he pronounced his work "very good." God did not create human beings as ghostlike creatures but as embodied souls. The resurrection of the body affirms the goodness of God's original creation, and recognizes that the basic human problem is not finitude but fallenness. It also declares that God will make good and bring to perfection the human project he began in the Garden of Eden.

The Incarnation teaches that the eternal Son of God entered so deeply into our human reality that he did not shun the virgin's womb, nor the evildoer's cross. This same one, Jesus Christ, also rose again in his body "on the third day."

Jesus' bodily resurrection is the guarantee of our own future resurrection. He rose literally, physically, historically, and in a body that was no less visible and tangible than those of his very earthy disciples, though remarkably transformed nonetheless. All of this gives us reason to hope that "when he appears, we shall be like him, for we shall see him as he is" (1 John 3:2). Despite the persistence of sin, death, and decay, we can live with confidence and hope that God's Kingdom will indeed come in a way that ends these miseries.

At Jesus' second coming, God will complete the restoration work he has already begun. He will redeem our bodies as well as our souls. Indeed, the entire cosmos will be gathered up in a new unity—that is, an ultimate healing, reconciliation, and bringing together of all things in Christ (Ephesians 1:10).

What will our resurrection bodies be like? This question was asked in 1 Corinthians 15:35. God does not give us a complete answer, but we do know that our new, glorified bodies will be imperishable. No more cancer, no more drownings, no more holocausts.

Our bodies will also be spiritual (Greek, *pneumatikos*). This word does not mean nonphysical, but rather bodies "transformed by and adapted to the new world of God's Spirit" (George E. Ladd). They also will be recognizable, but, like Jesus' risen body, so utterly transformed that we shall be aware of the differences as well as the sameness.

Most Christians believe that between death and the resurrection we shall indeed live in God's presence in conscious awareness of the Lord and others who have gone before us. This is wonderful, but it is not the end of the journey. In some ways, it is only the prelude to the main event that will begin in earnest on "that great getting-up morning" and that will include the new heavens and the new earth, the marriage banquet of the Lamb, the defanging of Satan, and the abolition of sin and sorrow forever.

TIMOTHY GEORGE is the founding dean of Beeson Divinity School and has been at Beeson since its inception in 1988. A prolific author, he has written more than twenty books and regularly contributes to scholarly journals. He has pastored churches in Tennessee, Alabama, and Massachusetts.

What Will Our Bodies Be Like?

J. OSWALD SANDERS—1993

PAUL IS RETICENT about going into detail about the exact nature of the resurrection body of the believer, probably because of the paucity of revealed facts. Yet he does make several very definite statements. About such subjects the philosopher and the scientist can make only educated guesses. With the inspired Word in our hands, however, we have certainty.

1. It will be a *spiritual* body (1 Corinthians 15:44), but will be perfectly adapted to our heavenly environment.
2. It will be a *real* body, not a phantom, but will be like that of the risen Christ, who challenged His disciples, "Touch me and see."
3. It will be a *recognizable* body, having identity with the physical body that has been laid to rest. After the resurrection Jesus spoke of having "flesh and bones." The Apostles recognized Jesus. . . .
4. It will be an *incorruptible* body (v. 42). It will be deathless, not subject to decay.
5. It will be a *glorious* body (v. 43), no longer "the body of our humiliation," subject to the tyranny of sin and the attacks of Satan.
6. It will be a *powerful* body (v. 43), having thrown off the frailty of its mortality.

While now the body is only an imperfect vehicle of the spirit and often frustrates it, in heaven the new body will be perfectly suited to conditions in its new sphere. "And just as we have borne the likeness of the earthly man, so shall we be the likeness of the man from heaven" (1 Corinthians 15:49). . . .

Our Lord's resurrection body is the pattern for ours. . . . When our Lord returns, a glorious transformation will be effected. Our lowly bodies will become like His *glorious* body, and will be bodies in which our longings and aspirations will find perfect expression.

J. Oswald Sanders, a native of New Zealand, was a consulting director of Overseas Missionary Fellowship and carried out an international preaching ministry. He was awarded the Order of the British Empire for Christian service and theological writing.

Our Glorified Body

John Wesley's 1732 revision of a sermon by Benjamin Calamy—1704

Oh when shall we arrive at that happy land where no complaints were ever heard, where we shall all enjoy uninterrupted health both of body and mind, and never more be exposed to any of those inconveniences that disturb our present pilgrimage! When we shall have once passed from death unto life, we shall be eased of all the troublesome care of our bodies, which now takes up so much of our time and thoughts. We shall be set free from all those mean and tiresome labours which we must now undergo to support our lives. Yon robes of light, with which we shall be clothed at the resurrection of the just, will not stand in need of those careful provisions which it is so troublesome to us here either to procure or to be without. But then, as our Lord tells us, "Those who shall be accounted worthy to obtain that world, neither marry nor are given in marriage, neither can they die any more, but they are equal to the angels." Their bodies are neither subject to disease, nor want that daily sustenance, which these mortal bodies cannot be without.

"Meats for the belly, and the belly for meats; but God will destroy both it and them." This is that perfect happiness which all good men shall enjoy in the other world. A mind free from all trouble and guilt, in a body free from all pains and diseases. Thus our mortal bodies shall be raised immortal. They shall not only be always preserved from death (for so these might be, if God pleased) but the nature of them shall be wholly changed, so that they shall not retain the same seeds of mortality: they cannot die any more.

This earthly body is slow and heavy in all its motions. . . .
But our heavenly bodies shall be as fire;
as active and as nimble as our thoughts are.

Our bodies shall he raised in glory. "Then shall the righteous shine as the sun in the kingdom of their Father." A resemblance of this we have in the lustre of Moses's face, when he had conversed with God on the mount. His face shone so bright, that the children of Israel were afraid to come near him, till he threw a veil over it. And that extraordinary majesty of Stephen's face, seemed to be an earnest of his glory. "All that sat in the council, looking steadfastly on him, saw his face as it had been the face of an angel." How then, if it shone so gloriously even on earth, will it shine in the other world, when his, and the bodies of all the saints, are made like unto Christ's glorious body! How glorious the body of Christ is, we may guess from his transfiguration. St. Peter, when he saw this, when our Lord's face shone as the sun, and his raiment became shining and white as snow, was so transported with joy and admiration, that he knew not what he said. When our Saviour discovered but a little of that glory which he now possesses, and which in due time he will impart to his followers, yet that little of it made the place seem a paradise; and the disciples thought, that they could wish for nothing better than always to live in such pure light, and enjoy so beautiful a sight. "It is good for us to be here: let us make three tabernacles." Here let us fix our abode for ever. And if they thought it so happy only to be present with such heavenly bodies, and to behold them with their eyes, how much happier must it be to dwell in such glorious mansions, and to be themselves clothed with so much brightness! . . .

Our bodies shall be raised in power. This expresses the sprightliness of our heavenly bodies, the nimbleness of their motion, by which they shall be obedient and able instruments of the soul. In this state, our bodies are no better than clogs and fetters, which confine and restrain the freedom of the soul. The corruptible body presses down the soul, and the earthly tabernacle weighs down the mind. Our dull, sluggish, inactive bodies, are often unable, or backward, to obey the commands of the soul. But in the other life, "they that wait upon the Lord shall renew their strength; they shall mount up with wings as eagles, they shall run and not be weary, they shall walk, and not faint." Or, as another expresses it, "they shall run to and fro like sparks among the stubble." The speed of their motion shall be like that of devouring fire in stubble, and the height of it above the towering of an eagle; for they shall meet the Lord in the air, when he comes to judgment, and mount up with him into the highest heaven. This earthly body is slow and heavy in all its motions, listless and soon tired with action. But our heavenly bodies shall be as fire; as active and as nimble as our thoughts are.

Our bodies shall be raised spiritual bodies. Our spirits are now forced to serve our bodies, and to attend their leisure, and do greatly depend upon them for most of their actions. But our bodies shall then wholly serve our spirits, and minister to them, and depend upon them. So that, as by a natural body, we understand one fitted for this lower, sensible world, for this earthly state; so a spiritual body is one that is suited to a spiritual state, to an invisible world, to the life of angels. And, indeed, this is the principal difference between a mortal and a glorified body. This flesh is the most dangerous enemy we have: we therefore deny and renounce it in our baptism. It constantly tempts us to evil. Every sense is a snare to us. All its lusts and appetites are inordinate. It is ungovernable, and often rebels against reason. The law in our members wars against the law of our mind. When the spirit is willing, the flesh is weak; so that the best of men are forced to keep it under, and use it hardly, lest it should betray them into folly and misery. And how does it hinder us in all our devotions! How soon does it jade our minds when employed on holy things! How easily by its enchanting pleasures, does it divert them from those noble exercises! But when we have obtained the resurrection unto life, our bodies will be spiritualized, purified, and refined from their earthly grossness; then they will be fit instruments for the soul in all its divine and heavenly employment; we shall not be weary of singing praises to God through infinite ages.

John Wesley (1703–1791), an Anglican clergyman, was the founder of the Methodist movement. The fifteenth of nineteen children of the rector of Epworth, Lincolnshire, he studied at Oxford, where he and a few friends formed the Holy Club. Their organized manner of Christian living earned the name "Methodists." But it was not till after serving as a missionary in the American colony of Georgia that he experienced the warmth of true conversion to Christ. Thereafter Wesley became a tireless preacher throughout Great Britain and the American colonies, eventually covering 250,000 miles on horseback preaching and organizing Methodist societies. In addition to his own sermons and other writings, he adapted and republished many books of other Christian writers, and revised this sermon from one published in 1704 by Dr. Benjamin Calamy, a London vicar.

Vessels of Honor

Origen—*circa* 230

Our flesh is supposed by ignorant men and unbelievers to be destroyed after death, in such a degree that it retains no relic at all of its former substance. We, however, who believe in its resurrection, understand that a change only has been produced by death, but that its substance certainly remains; and that by the will of its Creator, and at the time appointed, it will be restored to life; and that a second time a change will take place in it, so that what at first was flesh (formed) out of earthly soil, and was afterwards dissolved by death, and again reduced to dust and ashes ("For dust thou art," it is said, "and to dust shall thou return"), will be again raised from the earth, and shall after this, according to the merits of the indwelling soul, advance to the glory of a spiritual body.

Into this condition, then, we are to suppose that all this bodily substance of ours will be brought, when all things shall be re-established in a state of unity, and when God shall be all in all. And this result must be understood as being brought about, not suddenly, but slowly and gradually, seeing that the process of amendment and correction will take place imperceptibly in the individual instances during the lapse of countless and unmeasured ages, some outstripping others, and tending by a swifter course towards perfection, while others again follow close at hand, and some again a long way behind; and thus, through the numerous and uncounted orders of progressive beings who are being reconciled to God from a state of enmity, the last enemy is finally reached, who is called death, so that he also may be destroyed, and no longer be an enemy. When, therefore, all rational souls shall have been restored to a condition of this kind, then the nature of this body of ours will undergo a change into the glory of a spiritual body. For as we see it not to be the case with rational natures, that some of them have lived in a condition of degradation owing to their sins, while others have been called to a state of happiness on account of their merits; but as we see those same souls who had formerly been sinful, assisted, after their conversion and reconciliation to God, to a state of happiness; so also are we to consider, with respect to the nature of the body, that the one which we now make use of in a state of meanness, and corruption, and weakness, is not a different body from that which we shall possess in incorruption, and in power, and in glory; but that the same body, when it has cast away the infirmities in which it is now entangled, shall be transmuted into a condition of glory, being rendered spiritual, so that what was a vessel of dishonour may, when cleansed, become a vessel unto honour, and an abode of blessedness. And in this condition, also, we are to believe, that by the will of the Creator, it will abide for ever without any change, as is confirmed by the declaration of the apostle, when he says, "We have a house, not made with hands, eternal in the heavens." . . . The holy apostle manifestly declares, that it is not new bodies which are given to those who rise from the dead, but that they receive those identical ones which they had possessed when living, transformed from an inferior into a better condition. For his words are: "It is sown an animal body, it will rise a spiritual body; it is sown in corruption, it will arise in incorruption: it is sown in weakness, it will arise in power: it is sown in dishonour, it will arise in glory." As, therefore, there is a kind of advance in man, so that from being first an animal being, and not understanding what belongs to the Spirit of God, he reaches by means of instruction the stage of being made a spiritual being, and of judging all things, while he himself is judged by no one; so also, with respect to the state of the body, we are to hold that this very body which now, on account of its service to the soul, is styled an animal body, will, by means of a certain progress, when the soul, united to God, shall have been made one spirit with Him (the body even then ministering, as it were, to the spirit), attain to a spiritual condition and quality, especially since, as we have often pointed out, bodily nature was so formed by the Creator, as to pass easily into whatever condition he should wish, or the nature of the case demand.

ORIGEN (*circa* 185–254) was born into a Christian home in Alexandria, Egypt. When his father died in an attack on Christians, Origin was prevented from seeking martyrdom only because his mother hid his clothing. Still a layman, he became head of a Christian school in Alexandria, but was ordained after moving to Palestine in 230. He was a prolific author, but few of his works have survived because of their length and because later authorities objected to some of his ideas. Nevertheless, Origen is recognized as the ancient Greek-speaking church's most thorough biblical scholar. His most important theological work is *The Fundamental Doctrines* (Περι Ἀρχων or *De Principiis*). Origin died after being tortured in the persecution under the emperor Decius.

The Spiritual Body

R. C. SPROUL—1988

THE TERM *spiritual body* sounds discordant to the ear. We tend to think of spirit and body as mutually exclusive polar opposites. But Paul is not resorting to contradictions to make his point. He is referring to a spiritualized body that has been transformed from its natural limitations. It is a glorified body, a body that is raised in a new dimension.

The only real clue we have to this type of spiritual body is the sketchy view we have of the resurrected body of Jesus. We know that the body Jesus had after His resurrection was different from the body that was buried. It manifested both continuity and discontinuity. We read of people having some difficulty recognizing Him, yet, at the same time, recognition did occur. Jesus ate breakfast with His disciples. He showed the marks of His crucifixion to Thomas. . . .

John also records a cryptic statement about Jesus that has fueled much speculation about His resurrected body.

> *After eight days His disciples were again inside, and Thomas with them. Jesus came, the doors being shut, and stood in the midst, and said, "Peace to you!" (John 20:26 NASB)*

Why does John record the phrase "the doors being shut"? Is the phrase included to tell us something about the disciples, or to tell us something about the resurrected body of Jesus? . . .

We can possibly reconstruct the scene in this way: The disciples, in a state of fright, were huddled together with the door shut. While they were preoccupied with their fear and consternation, Jesus came to their place of assembly, quietly opened the door, and came in and spoke to them. In this scenario the reference to the shut door tells us nothing about the resurrected body of Jesus other than it could walk around and open doors.

On the other hand, perhaps John is hinting that Jesus appeared in the middle of the room *without* opening the door. This would mean that His resurrected body had the capacity to move unimpeded through solid objects. . . .

What is certain is that Paul looks to Jesus as the exemplar of what our resurrected bodies will be like:

> *And so it is written, "The first man Adam became a living being." The last Adam became a life-giving spirit. However, the spiritual is not first, but the natural, and afterward the*

> *spiritual. The first man was of the earth, made of dust; the second Man is the Lord from heaven. As was the man of dust, so also are those who are made of dust; and as is the heavenly Man, so also are those who are heavenly. And as we have borne the image of the man of dust, we shall also bear the image of the heavenly Man.* (1 Corinthians 15:45–49 NASB)

All we who are human partake of the earthly nature of Adam. We are children of the dust. Our bodies suffer from all the weaknesses and frailties that belong to the earth. Our new natures will involve a tabernacle made in heaven. In the heavenly body there is no room for cancer or heart disease. The curse of the fall will be removed. We will be clothed after the image and likeness of the New Adam, the heavenly Man. We will still be men. There will be continuity. Our personal identities will remain intact. We will be recognizable as the persons we are. But there will also be discontinuity as the shackles of the dust will be liberated by the heavenly form.

For biographical information on this author, see page 12.

The Honor of Our New Bodies

MARTIN LUTHER— *circa* 1530

WE ARE NO LONGER citizens of earth. The baptized Christian is born a citizen of heaven through baptism. We should be mindful of this fact and walk here as if native there. We are to console ourselves with the fact that God thus accepts us and will transplant us there. Meantime we must await the coming again of the Saviour, who is to bring from heaven to us eternal righteousness, life, honor and glory.

We are baptized and made Christians, not to the end that we may have great honor, or renown of righteousness, or earthly dominion, power and possessions. Notwithstanding we do have these because they are requisite to our physical life, yet we are to regard them as mere filth, wherewith we minister to our bodily welfare as best we can for the benefit of posterity. We Christians, however, are expectantly to await the coming of the Saviour. His coming will not be to our injury or shame as it may be in the case of others. He comes for the salvation of our unprofitable, impotent bodies. Wretchedly worthless as they are in this life, they are much more unprofitable when lifeless and perishing in the earth.

Christ will at his coming render our bodies beautiful, pure, shining and worthy of honor, until they correspond to his own immortal, glorious body.

But, however miserable, powerless and contemptible in life and death, Christ will at his coming render our bodies beautiful, pure, shining and worthy of honor, until they correspond to his own immortal, glorious body. Not like it as it hung on the cross or lay in the grave, bloodstained, livid and disgraced; but as it is now, glorified at the Father's right hand. We need not, then, be alarmed at the necessity of laying aside our earthly bodies; at being despoiled of the honor, righteousness and life adhering in them, to deliver it to the devouring power of death and the grave—something well calculated to terrify the enemies of Christ: but we may joyfully hope for and await his speedy coming to deliver us from this miserable, filthy pollution. "According to the working whereby he is able even to subdue all things unto himself."

Think of the honor and the glory Christ's righteousness brings even to our bodies! How can this poor, sinful, miserable, filthy, polluted body become like unto that of the Son of God, the Lord of Glory? What are you—your powers and abilities, or those of all men, to effect this glorious thing? But Paul says human righteousness, merit, glory and power have nothing to do with it. They are mere filth and pollution, and condemned as well. Another force intervenes, the power of Christ the Lord, who is able to bring all things into subjection to himself. Now, if he has power to subject all things unto himself at will, he is also able to glorify the pollution and filth of this wretched body, even when it has become worms and dust. In his hands it is as clay in the hands of the potter, and from the polluted lump of clay he can make a vessel that shall be a beautiful, new, pure, glorious body, surpassing the sun in its brilliance and beauty.

Through baptism Christ has taken us into his hands, actually that he may exchange our sinful, condemned, perishable, physical lives for the new, imperishable righteousness and life he prepares for body and soul. Such is the power and the agency exalting us to marvelous glory—something no earthly righteousness of the Law could accomplish. The righteousness of the Law leaves our bodies to shame and destruction; it reaches not beyond physical existence. But the righteousness of Christ inspires with power, making evident that we worship not the body but the true and living God, who does not leave us to shame and destruction, but delivers from sin, death and condemnation, and exalts this perishable body to eternal honor and glory.

MARTIN LUTHER (1483–1546), founder of the German Reformation, was ordained a priest in 1507 and then appointed to the faculty of the University of Wittenberg, where he remained a professor till his death. Anxiety about his salvation caused him to question the practice of church authorities' dispensing indulgences, or forgiveness of the penalty of sin. His 95 Theses or objections of 1517 led to a series of disputes with church authorities, but Luther enjoyed the favor of the prince of Saxony and, during a protective imprisonment, was able to translate the Bible into German. Breaking with the Roman Church, he instituted reforms in Wittenberg, but others carried Luther's ideas to more radical extremes as the Reformation spread. Luther's voluminous writings reveal him as a complex personality aware of the depth of sin and the need for grace alone as the way to salvation.

Trusting

L. D. JOHNSON—1978

BEYOND HIS CARING and the understanding he has shared with us, Jesus has done one other thing. He asks us to trust him and our heavenly Father as we deal with death. Where we cannot understand he bids us believe. What a terrifying world it would be if we could trust no one, depend upon no one's veracity and motive. Jesus asks us to believe in the trustworthiness of the Father. "If you then, though you are evil, know how to give good gifts to your children, how much more will your Father in heaven give good gifts to those who ask him!" (Matthew 7:11). If human fathers may be trusted, how much more the heavenly Father!

Jesus' own example of trust encourages us. In the garden of Gethsemane he asked that he might be spared the suffering of the cross and death, but he concluded that prayer with an expression of complete confidence in the purpose and goodness of God: "Nevertheless not as I will, but as thou wilt" (Matthew 26:39 KJV). And as he hung dying upon the cross he reaffirmed that confidence when he said, "Father, into Thy hands I commit my spirit."

James Gordon Gilkey has related in a sermon a touching story about a nineteenth-century Congregational minister of New England, named John Todd. Left an orphan when he was six, John Todd had been reared by an aunt who had seen him through Yale and divinity school. During Todd's pastorate in Pittsfield, Massachusetts, he received a pitiful letter from his aged aunt, telling him in great distress that her doctor had told her that she was the victim of an incurable disease and that death was not only inevitable but imminent. He had been to college and seminary; he had read books and was wise. Could he tell her about death? Was there anything to fear?

This was John Todd's answer: "It is now thirty-five years since I a little boy of six, was left quite alone in the world. You sent me word you would give me a home and be a kind mother to me. I have never forgotten the day when I made the long journey of ten miles from my home in Killingworth to your home in North Killingworth. I can still recall my disappointment when I learned that instead of coming for me yourself you had sent your colored man Caesar to fetch me. I can still remember my tears and anxiety as, perched on your horse and clinging tight to Caesar, I started for my new home."

Then Todd went on to describe his childish anxiety as darkness fell before the journey was ended and how he wondered if his aunt would have gone to bed before he got there. Presently, he wrote, they had ridden out of the woods into a clearing and his aunt was waiting at the door. He remembered her warm arms around him, lifting him gently—a tired and bewildered little boy—down from the horse. She had given him supper beside the bright fire in her hearth and then had taken him to his room and sat beside him till he dropped off to sleep.

"You are probably wondering why I am now recalling all these things to your mind," he added. "Some day soon God will send for you, to take you to a new home. Don't fear the summons, the strange journey, the messenger of death. At the end of the road you will find love and a welcome; you will be safe in God's care and keeping. God can be trusted—trusted to be as kind to you as you were to me so many years ago."

God can be trusted! In the last analysis, Christians have no more persuasive word. God can be trusted. That does not resolve all the mysteries or answer all the questions, but it gives us enough to build our lives around. God is trustworthy. He is Lord of life and death, and he is to be trusted. "Let not your hearts be troubled," Jesus said, "believe!"

L. D. JOHNSON (1916–1981) was chaplain and professor of religion at Furman University in Greenville, South Carolina, from 1967 until his death in 1981. He wrote numerous articles and books, besides a weekly religious column for several newspapers with a combined circulation of more than 200,000.

To Be with Christ

CHARLES HADDON SPURGEON—1859

"In vain the fancy strives to paint
The moment after death;
The glories which surround the saint
When yielding up his breath.
This much—and this is all we know,
They are supremely blest;
Have done with sin, and care, and woe,
And with their Saviour rest."

Chapter 5

THIS IS PRECISELY THE APOSTLE'S DESCRIPTION of the state of the believer after death. They depart; yes, but whither? To be with Christ. Just observe how quickly these scenes follow each other. The sail is spread; the soul is launched upon the deep. How long will be its voyage? How many wearying winds must beat upon the sail ere it shall be reefed in the port of peace? How often shall that soul be tossed upon the waves before it comes to the sea that knows no storm. Oh tell it, tell it everywhere; yon ship that has just departed is already at its haven. It did but spread its sail and it was there. Like the old ship on the lake of Galilee, there was a storm that tossed it, but Jesus said, "Peace, be still," and immediately it came to land. Yes, think not that there is a long period between the instant of death and the eternity of glory. There is not so much as space for the intervening of a lightning's flash. One gentle sigh, the fetter breaks, we scarce can say it is gone before the ransomed spirit takes its mansion near the throne. We depart, we are with Christ; more quickly than I can say the words, swifter than speech can express them they become true. They depart, now they are with Christ; the selfsame instant they have closed their eyes on earth they have opened them in heaven. And what is this invisible part of death? *"To be with Christ."* Who can comprehend this but the Christian? It is a heaven which the worldling cares not for, if he could have it, he would not pawn his meanest lust to gain it. To be with Christ is to him a thing of nought, as gold and silver are of no more value to little children than the pieces of platter with which they will amuse themselves. So heaven and being with Christ is of no value to the childish sons of earthly mirth. They know not what a mass of glory is crowded into that one sentence. "To be with Christ." To the believer who understands it, it means, first, *vision.* "Thine eyes shall see him." I have heard of *him,* and though I have not seen his face, unceasingly I have adored him. But I shall *see* him. Yes, we shall actually gaze upon the exalted Redeemer. Realize the thought. Is there not a young heaven within it? Thou shalt see the hand that was nailed for thee; thou shalt kiss the very lips that said, "I thirst"; thou shalt see the thorn-crowned head, and bow with all the blood-washed throng, thou, the chief of sinners, shalt adore him who washed thee in his blood; when thou shalt have a vision of his glory. Faith is precious but what must sight be? To view Jesus as the Lamb of God through the glass of faith makes the soul rejoice with joy unspeakable; but oh! to see him face to face, to look into those dear eyes; to be embraced by those divine arms—rapture begins at the very mention of it! While I speak of him, my soul is like the chariots of Aminadab, and I desire to depart and to be with him. But what must the vision be when the veil is taken from his face, and the dimness from our eyes, and when we shall talk with him even as a man talketh with his friend. But it is not only vision, it is *communion*. We shall walk with him, he shall walk with us, he shall speak to us, and we shall speak to him. All that the spouse desired in Solomon's Song, we shall have, and ten thousand times more. Then will the prayer be fulfilled "Let him kiss me with the kisses of his lips, for his love is better than wine." Then we shall be able to say "His left hand is under my head, and his right hand doth embrace me." Then will he tell us his love; then will rehearse the ancient story of the everlasting covenant, of his election of us by his own true love, of his bethrothal of us through his boundless affection, of his purchase of us by his rich compassion, of his preservation of us by his omnipotence, and of his bringing us safe at last to glory as the result of his promise and his blood. And then will we tell to him our love, then into his ear will we pour out the song of gratitude, a song such as we have never sung on earth, unmixed and pure, full of serenity and joy, no groans to mar its melody; a song rapt and seraphic, like the flaming sonnets which flash from burning tongues above. Happy, happy, happy day, when vision and communion shall be ours in fullness! "To be with Christ which is far better."

Charles Haddon Spurgeon (1834–1892), legendary English preacher, received much of his religious training from his father and grandfather, both of whom were preachers. A Calvinist and Baptist, he preached for thirty-eight years at the Metropolitan Tabernacle in London to audiences that frequently numbered in excess of ten thousand. He wrote more than 3,560 sermons, along with commentaries, devotions, and other works.

CHAPTER 6

Loved Ones in Heaven

Shall We Know One Another?

J. PATERSON-SMYTH—1910

SHALL WE KNOW ONE ANOTHER IN THAT LIFE? Why not? As George MacDonald somewhere pertinently asks, "Shall we be greater fools in Paradise than we are here?"

This is a perfectly apt retort, and not at all flippant as it may seem at first. It is based on the belief suggested by common sense and confirmed by Scripture that our life there will be the natural continuous development of our life here and not some utterly unconnected existence. If consciousness, personal identity, character, love, memory, fellowship, intercourse go on in that life why should there be a question raised about recognition? True, there are morbid times with most of us when we are inclined to doubt all desirable things, and there are some gloomy Christians who are always suspicious of anything especially bright and hopeful in the Gospel of Christ. But to the normal Christian man who knows what is revealed and who believes in the love of God, there should never be any serious doubt about recognition in that life. . . .

I wonder if anybody really doubts it after all. Just think of it! With Christ in Paradise and not knowing or loving any comrade soul! Is that possible in the land of love? With our dear ones in Paradise and never a thrill of recognition as we touch in spiritual intercourse the mother, or wife, or husband, or child for whose presence we are longing! Cannot you imagine our wondering joy when our questionings are set at rest?

Cannot you imagine the Lord in His tender reproach, "Oh, thou of little faith, wherefore didst thou doubt?" . . .

If we shall not know one another, why is there this undying memory of departed ones, the aching void that is never filled on earth?

We know that Heaven would scarce be Heaven at all if we were to be but solitary isolated spirits amongst a crowd of others whom we did not know or love. We know that the next world and this world come from the same God who is the same always. We know that in this world He has bound us up in groups, knowing and loving and sympathizing with each other. Unless His method utterly changes He must do the same hereafter. And we have seen what a prophecy of recognition lies deep in the very fibres of that nature which God has implanted in us. If we shall not know one another, why is there this undying memory of departed ones, the aching void that is never filled on earth? The lower animals lose their young and in a few days forget them. But the poor, human mother never forgets. When her head is bowed with age, when she has forgotten nearly all else on earth, you can bring the tears into her eyes by mentioning the child that died in her arms forty years ago. Did God implant that divine love in her only to disappoint it? God forbid! A thousand times, no. In that world the mother shall meet her child, and the lonely widow shall meet her husband, and they shall learn fully the love of God in that rapturous meeting with Christ's benediction resting on them.

I know there are further questions rising in our hearts. Will our dear ones remember us? Will they, in all the years of progress, have grown too good and great for fellowship with us? There is no specific answer save what we can infer from the boundless goodness and kindness of God. Since He does not forget us we may be sure they will not forget us. Since His superior greatness and holiness does not put Him beyond our reach, we may be sure that theirs will not—their growth will be mainly a growth of love which will only bring them closer to us for ever and ever.

John Paterson-Smyth (1852–1932), born in Ireland, was an Anglican minister and professor of pastoral theology at the University of Dublin. Emigrating to Canada, he served for nineteen years as rector of St. George's Church, Montreal. He wrote twenty books on biblical and other subjects.

Reunion in Heaven

Charles Wesley—1759

Come, let us join our friends above
That have obtained the prize,
And on the eagle wings of love
To joys celestial rise:
Let all the saints terrestrial sing,
With those to glory gone;
For all the servants of our King,
In earth and heaven, are one.

One family we dwell in him,
One church, above, beneath,
Though now divided by the stream,
The narrow stream of death:
One army of the living God,
To his command we bow;
Part of his host have crossed the flood,
And part are crossing now.

Ten thousand to their endless home
This solemn moment fly;
And we are to the margin come,
And we expect to die:
His militant embodied host,
With wishful looks we stand,
And long to see that happy coast,
And reach the heavenly land.

Our old companions in distress
We haste again to see,
And eager long for our release,
And full felicity:
Even now by faith we join our hands
With those that went before;
And greet the blood-besprinkled bands
On the eternal shore.

Our spirits too shall quickly join,
Like theirs with glory crowned,
And shout to see our Captain's sign,
To hear his trumpet sound.
O that we now might grasp our guide!
O that the word were given!
Come, Lord of hosts, the waves divide,
And land us all in heaven!

Charles Wesley (1707–1788), Anglican clergyman, was a co-worker with his brother John in the early Methodist movement. England's most gifted and prolific hymn writer, he wrote the words to more than 5,500 hymns. Many remain in common use, such as "Jesus, Lover of My Soul," "Love Divine, All Loves Excelling," and "Hark! The Herald Angels Sing."

Heaven Is a Populated Place

Dr. Tony Evans—2000

Just in case you are worried about being a little lonely in heaven, let me show you some of the crowd that is going to share heaven with you. Hebrews 12:22–23 says, "You have come to Mount Zion and to the city of the living God, the heavenly Jerusalem, and to myriads of angels, to the general assembly and church of the firstborn who are enrolled in heaven, and to God, the

Judge of all, and to the spirits of the righteous made perfect" (NASB).

The writer of Hebrews . . . said the church of Jesus Christ will be in heaven, all those who have put their trust in Christ for salvation. So your spiritual family will be there.

In heaven all the masks and the pretense will be removed, and we will know each other as God created us to be.

One of our church members asked me if we will know each other once we get to heaven. The answer is that we won't really know each other *until* we get to heaven. Why? Because we cannot fully know each other now. All I can know about other people is what I see and what they tell me. And that's not all there is to a person. But in heaven all the masks and the pretense will be removed, and we will know each other as God created us to be.

Another group of people in heaven is the Old Testament saints, called "the spirits of the righteous made perfect" (Hebrews 12:23).

You'll be able to go down to the corner of Gold Street and Silver Boulevard, run into Abraham, and ask him a few questions. David can tell you the story of how he killed Goliath. You can ask Jonah what it felt like to be swallowed by a fish and live inside of it for three days.

You'll be in heaven with all of these people because heaven is a populated place. God created it to be inhabited.

For biographical information on this author, see page 30.

Bonded with the Departed

F. R. Anspach—1854

While ostensibly there is a gulf between [the living and the departed] so wide and deep that neither could venture to cross it, that bond of union which [makes] them members of the same family reaches across that gulf; and do what they may, they cannot annihilate that affection which they bear to each other. . . .

There are innumerable instances where such barriers interpose, that all personal intercourse is broken off between those of the same household; but though they should even desire to extinguish their love for those who are joined to them by ties of consanguinity, they shall not be able to do it. It is a law of their nature, and they must yield submission to its dictates. There is a father whose wishes have been thwarted concerning a beloved, perhaps idolized, child, whose disobedience to parental authority has banished her from his home and presence; but although there may be a coolness and determinateness of aspect on his brow, and an inflexible sternness may mantle his features, which would exclude the disobedient one from his house, yet, notwithstanding that forbidding exterior, that daughter has a home in his heart; and in secret he deplores her in all the bitterness of his soul. A kind Providence has, therefore, made a glorious provision, and placed it in our spiritual constitution with which to arm us against those calamities and changes which are incident to our earthly pilgrimage. We are united to those we love by eternal bonds. They may pass away from the earth, and we may commit their bodies to the tomb; but this bond reaches beyond the sepulchre, and holds them in sweet embrace. Such a view is certainly not opposed to the teachings of the Scriptures, and is in strict conformity with the laws of our being, and the testimony of our inward consciousness. We are just as cognizant of the fact that we love our sainted friends, as we are that we affectionately cherish our fellow-pilgrims on earth. There is not a day that we do not hold communion with them, and they with us. For it is our privilege to believe that our departed are interested in our welfare, and perhaps permitted to attend us, and to minister to us in our upward progress to eternal life. While they are elevated in their views and feelings above the possibility of experiencing pain (supposing them to be cognizant of our infirmities and imperfections), they may be round and about us, and render important service in the work of our salvation. But whatever the offices may be with which they are charged, we rejoice in the assurances of our hearts that the flow of affection between us and them continues in a current that is ever deepening and widening as we are progressing towards our eternal home. The indestructibility of this bond of family union is a gracious and exhaustless source of consolation to the children of God, and a conviction to which the soul clings with all its immortal energies. This thought is beautifully expanded in some stanzas by Wordsworth, in a dialogue with a little girl whom he interrogates as to the number of their family.

> "Sisters and brothers, little Maid,
> How many may you be?"
> "How many? seven in all," she said,
> And wondering looked at me.
> "And where are they, I pray you tell?"
> She answered, "Seven are we,
> And two of us at Conway dwell,
> And two are gone to sea.
> Two of us in the churchyard lie—
> My sister and my brother;
> And in the churchyard cottage, I
> Dwell near them with my mother."
> "But they are dead; those two are dead!
> Their spirits are in heaven!"
> 'Twas throwing words away: for still
> The little Maid would have her will,
> And said, "Nay, we are seven."

No poet, ay, no philosopher could have changed her mind, for none could reason out of existence this family bond. They were seven; two were at sea, two at Conway, two were slumbering in the grave, and she was living with her mother—like the billows of the deep, which are distinct and many, yet form but one ocean.

It is a blessed thought that we shall still love in heaven, and experience joy in the society of dear departed ones. How cheering the knowledge, while toiling through the world as strangers and pilgrims, that the bond of affection which unites us to hearts throbbing with the same high impulses, and animated with the same immortal hopes which thrill within us, is to last forever! And if we have beloved parents, brothers, sisters, companions, or children amid the glorious realities of that immortal state where one instant is worth all the concentrated delights of earth, we are linked by the strongest and tenderest ties to those amazing blessings which are at the right hand of God. Christianity throws a grandeur around the prospects of the believer, so dazzling that an angel might sink in silent wonder and admiration before it. And what motives do these considerations furnish to rear our children for heaven! If we attune infant lips to praise, those notes of thanksgiving will vibrate forever. If the moulding hand of the Redeemer is drawn upon them, and the Holy Spirit teaches their hearts to make melody to the Lord, those melodies will be heard when the music of the spheres shall be silent. And O! what rapture will spread through the entire circle, when all the members of our family shall have reached those blissful shores! Who can imagine what we shall feel, when it can be said we are all in heaven! When the last wanderer has come in with songs of deliverance, and the shout rings through the armies of the redeemed—all home, home from the distant land—forever home! Let us rejoice in this union of hearts. Let us bless God for making the family bond durable as the soul. O! my sainted mother! my beloved sister! my beautiful angel boy, I will not deplore you as lost; for ye are still ours, we are yet one, and shall forever be, for that bond which unites us shall exist in all its vigor when the wheels of the universe stand still! When every mountain shall have fallen, it shall stand unimpaired; when every law whose authority is acknowledged by material nature shall have been annulled, this law which makes us one, shall be in force. When every river has run dry, and the sea is without a drop, this family bond shall roll through the immense channels of our immortal being, streams of glory. This assurance of the indestructibility of the family bond, fills even the grief-stricken with ecstacy [*sic*], and sheds gleams of eternal sunshine upon the life, dark with afflictive bereavements. And is there not a depth of consolation in this, which should reanimate with joy those desolate souls which are wasting away in sighs of grief! Come to the cross, ye mourning and afflicted ones; gather around the bleeding sacrifice of Calvary; steep those hearts in atoning blood, until, washed and purified, they become the habitation of the Holy Ghost, and he will give birth to such hopes as will shed a sweet peace over your wounded and weary spirits, while they will raise you into communion with the saints on high. And if we are exalted into fellowship with the Father and the Son, we shall finally ascend to the presence of God, "where there is fulness of joy, and to his right hand where there are pleasures forevermore."

Frederick Reinhart Anspach (1815–1867) was a noted preacher of his time in German Reformed and Lutheran circles. He was a pastor in Hagerstown, Maryland, then in Baltimore, where he edited the *Lutheran Observer.* His first publication was a sermon delivered on the death of Henry Clay, followed in rapid succession by a number of books.

Kinship That Lasts

Valerie Fraser—2000

My mother and her four brothers and sisters have spent many a Sunday afternoon trying to figure out if they'll know each other in heaven.

It's a matter of considerable concern.

Over the years, these close-knit siblings have weathered the loss of many loved ones. Each time, they have overcome the pain of separation by joining hands in an unshakable bond of family unity and holding fast to their faith. For those who remain on this earthly bank of Jordan, the very notion that they might not recognize each other on the other side is unthinkable.

"The Bible says we will all be changed," a troubled aunt says, her voice rising with that last worrisome word. "Yes, but it also says we shall know as we are known." A reassuring uncle counters. My mother settles the question in her own decisive way. "Well, I just believe we're gonna *know* each other. Who wants coffee?"

I'm with Mother. Maybe it comes from growing up in a big Southern clan whose stories of the past are an integral part of every family dinner. Or maybe it's the cottonfields farmed by four generations, the kinship with all the other hands that have tended this earth. More than anything, I think it's the almost tangible presence I feel whenever I sit quietly on the rickety front porch of the old homeplace—long empty—or stand outside the small iron fence that surrounds my grandparents' graves. These are moments not of sadness, but of communion.

Never was that connection stronger than at the end of my maternal grandmother's 96 years. In her comfortable room in my parents' house, she was watched over both day and night by her daughters and daughters-in-law. Her sons were at her side every day, her grandchildren and great-grandchildren constantly about. It was a difficult time of letting go. And yet, there were moments of wonder and mystery, of comfort and joy.

Sometimes she would stop in mid-sentence, calmly point to a corner of her bedroom, and say "Why, there's Adam again—he was here this morning."

Adam was her younger brother who had died years before. Now and again, she would look heavenward and have a matter-of-fact conversation with someone unseen. It was as if she were talking on the telephone, and we could hear only her responses, not the message coming through from the other side.

Aunt Vivian joked about the spookiness of it. "When you're sitting up with Mother and she starts talking to those folks at two in the morning, you go to looking over your shoulder!"

I've thought about those visions a lot over the years, especially when my aunts and uncles are debating their heavenly identities. The visits from her late brother and the conversations with the great beyond were so real and comforting to my grandmother that they became real to us. They comforted us too.

Defying logic, they assured us that the ties of kinship really do last forever. For we knew that there, among us, in my grandmother's room was a band of family angels, comin' for to carry her home.

VALERIE FRASER is an Alabama native and holds degrees from Auburn University and Baylor University. She is the Creative Development Director of *Southern Living* magazine.

Chapter 6

They Serve in Fuller Life

William C. Piggott—1915

For those we love within the veil,
Who once were comrades of our way,
We thank Thee, Lord; for they have won
To cloudless day;

And life for them is life indeed,
The splendid goal of earth's strait race;
And where no shadows intervene
They see Thy face.

Not as we knew them any more,
Toil-worn, and sad with burden'd care:
Erect, clear-eyed, upon their brows
Thy Name they bear.

Free from the fret of mortal years,
And knowing now Thy perfect will,
With quickened sense and heightened joy,
They serve thee still.

O fuller, sweeter is that life,
And larger, ampler is the air:
Eye cannot see nor heart conceive
The glory there;

Nor know to what high purpose thou
Dost yet employ their ripened powers,
Nor how at thy behest they touch
This life of ours.

There are no tears within their eyes;
With love they keep perpetual tryst;

And praise and work and rest are one
With thee, O Christ.

William Charter Piggott (1872–1943) was pastor of several churches in England, including Whitefield's Tabernacle in London, and for twenty years the Streatham (London) Congregational Church, during which time he chaired the Congregational Union of England and Wales for a year.

If Resurrection, Then Heaven

Lee Strobel—1998

I had already made plane reservations for a trip to the other side of the country to interview one more expert on the final category of proof that the Resurrection is a real event of history.

Before I left [Prof. Gary] Habermas's office, however, I had one more question. Frankly, I hesitated to ask it, because it was a bit too predictable and I thought I'd get an answer that was a little too pat.

The question concerned the importance of the Resurrection. I figured if I asked Habermas about that, he'd give the standard reply about being at the center of Christian doctrine, the axis around which the Christian faith turned. And I was right—he did give a stock answer like that.

But what surprised me was that this wasn't all he said. This nuts-and-bolts scholar, this burly and straight-shooting debater, this combat-ready defender of the faith, allowed me to peer into his soul as he gave an answer that grew out of the deepest valley of despair he had ever walked through.

Habermas rubbed his graying beard. The quick-fire cadence and debater's edge to his voice were gone. No more quoting of scholars, no more citing of Scripture, no more building a case. I had asked about the importance of the Resurrection, and Habermas decided to take a risk by harkening back to 1995, when his wife, Debbie, slowly died of stomach cancer. Caught off guard by the tenderness of the moment, all I could do was listen.

"I sat on our porch," he began, looking off to the side at nothing in particular. He sighed deeply, then went on. "My wife was upstairs dying. Except for a few weeks, she was home through it all. It was an awful time. This was the worst thing that could possibly happen."

He turned and looked straight at me. "But do you know what was amazing? My students would call me—not just one but several of them—and say, 'At a time like this, aren't you glad about the Resurrection?' As sober as those circumstances were, I had to smile for two reasons. First, my students were trying to cheer me up with my own teaching. And second, it worked.

"As I would sit there, I'd picture Job, who went through all that terrible stuff and asked questions of God, but then God turned the tables and asked *him* a few questions.

"I knew if God were to come to me, I'd ask only one question: 'Lord, why is Debbie up there in bed?' And I think God would respond by asking gently, 'Gary, did I raise my Son from the dead?'

"I'd say, 'Come on, Lord, I've written seven books on that topic! Of course he was raised from the dead. But I want to know about Debbie!'

"I think he'd keep coming back to the same question—'Did I raise my Son from the dead?' 'Did I raise my Son from the dead?'—until I got his point: the Resurrection says that if Jesus was raised two thousand years ago, there's an answer to Debbie's death in 1995. And do you know what? It worked for me while I was sitting on the porch, and it still works today.

"It was a horribly emotional time for me, but I couldn't get around the fact that the Resurrection *is* the answer for her suffering. I still worried; I still wondered what I'd do raising four kids alone. But there wasn't a time when that truth didn't comfort me.

"Losing my wife was the most painful experience I've ever had to face, but if the Resurrection could get me through that, it can get me through anything. It was good for 30 A.D., it's good for 1995, it's good for 1998, and it's good beyond that."

Habermas locked eyes with mine. "That's not some sermon," he said quietly. "I believe that with all my heart. If there's a resurrection, there's a heaven. If Jesus was raised, Debbie was raised. And I will be someday, too.

"Then I'll see them both."

LEE STROBEL, with a Master of Studies in Law Degree from Yale Law School, was an award-winning journalist at the *Chicago Tribune*—and an atheist. After serving at Willow Creek Community Church and Saddleback Church, today this former spiritual skeptic concentrates his energies on writing. Lee is the author of numerous books.

Harmonies Fulfilled in Heaven

RALPH EMERSON BROWNS—1965

O why must war so soon destroy the bond
That love so lately hallowed, with but time
To sound, of all the music in our souls,
One chord that else had been a symphony?
Must I be satisfied that with a host
I share such grief as centuries have brought,
With Grecian maidens after Marathon
And Norman brides who mourned their gallant knights?

O God, there must be something more for us,
If love be not the grimmest jest of life.
The veil that keeps us from the holy place
Must have its rending at my hour of death,
And love, secure at last from damning strife,
Fulfill its harmonies in joyous life.

RALPH EMERSON BROWNS was a Methodist minister and professor at Illinois Wesleyan University. For a number of years he edited *The New Dictionary of Thoughts,* which was begun in the 1800s and is still being published.

Chapter 6

"Husband and Wife" in Heaven?

GEORGE MACDONALD—1880

THAT WINTER THE OLD PEOPLE were greatly tried with rheumatism; for not only were the frosts severe, but there was much rain between. Their children did all in their power to minister to their wants, and Gibbie was nurse as well as shepherd. . . . It was part of his business, as nurse, to keep up a good fire on the hearth; peats, happily, were plentiful. Awake for this cause, he heard in the middle of one night, the following dialogue between the husband and wife.

"I'm growin' terribly old, Janet," said Robert. "It's a sorry thing, this old age, and I can't make myself content with it. You see I haven't been used to it."

"That's true, Robert," answered Janet. "If we had been born old, we might by this time have been at home with it! But then what would have come of the grand delight of seein' old age run hobblin' away from the face of the Ancient of Days?". . .

"Eh! but I wish I may have you there, Janet, for I don't know what I would do in want of you. I would be mighty lost up yonder, if I had to go my path without you to refer to, that knows the ways of the place."

"I know no more about the ways of the place than yourself, Robert, though I'm thinkin' they'll be unusually quiet and reasonable, seein' that all there must be gentle folk. It's enough to me that I'll be in the house of my Master's Father; and my Master was well content to go to that house. And it must be something out of the ordinary, that was fit for him. But poor simple folk like ourselves will have no need to hang down the head and look like half-wits that don't know manners. Children are not expected to know all the ways of a big house that they have never been in before in their lives."

"It's not that altogether that troubles me, Janet; it's more that I'll be expected to sing and look pleased-like, and I don't know how it'll be possible, with you not bein' within my sight or my cry, or the hearin' of my ears."

"Do you believe this, Robert—that we're all one, just one, in Christ Jesus?"

"I can't well say. I'm not denyin' anything that the book tells me; you know me better than that, Janet. But there's many a thing it says that I don't know whether I believe it at my own hand, or whether it be only a thing that you believe, Janet. It's just to me as if I believed it myself; and that's a sorry thought, for a man can't be saved even by the proxy of his own wife."

"Well, you're just much where I find myself now, Robert; and I comfort myself with the hope that we'll know the thing there, that maybe we're but tryin' to believe here. But at any rate you have proved well that you and me's one, Robert. Now we know from Scripture that the Master came to make forever one, of them that was two. And we know also that he conquered Death. So he would never let Death make the one that he had made one into two again. There's no reason to think it! For all I know, what looks like a goin' away may be a comin' nearer. And there may be ways of comin' nearer to one another up yonder that we know nothing about down here.". . .

"Hoot, Janet! you know there's neither marryin' nor givin' in marriage there."

"Who was sayin' anything about marryin' or givin' in marriage, Robert? Is that to say that you and me's to be no more to one another than other folk? We wouldn't say, now would we, that just 'cause marriage is not the way of the country, there's to be nothing better in the place of it!"

"What made the Master say anything about it, then?"

"Just 'cause they plagued him with questions. He would never have opened his mouth about it—it wasn't one of his subjects. But then a few pride-bedecked book folk—that didn't believe there was any angels, or spirits of any kind, but said that a man once dead was forever and altogether dead, and yet pretended to believe in God himself for all that—thought to vex the Master with askin' which of seven that a poor body, that had been forced to marry them all, would be the wife of, when they got up again."

"A body might think it would be left to herself to say," suggested

Robert. "She had come through enough to have some claim to be considered!"

"She must have been a right good one," said Janet, "if each one of the seven would be wantin' her again. But I warrant she knew well enough which of them was her own!"

For biographical information on this author, see page 40.

Little Ones in Heaven

AUTHOR UNKNOWN—NINETEENTH CENTURY

Mid the pastures green of the blessed isles,
    Where never is heat or cold,
Where the light of life is the Shepherd's smile,
    Are the lambs of the Upper Fold.
Where the lilies blossom in fadeless spring,
    And never a heart grows old,
Where the glad new song is the song they sing,
    Are the lambs of the Upper Fold.
There are tiny mounds where the hopes of earth,
    Were laid 'neath the tear-wet mould,
But the light that paled at the stricken hearth,
    Was joy to the Upper Fold:
Oh, the white stone beareth a new name now,
    That never on earth was told,
And the tender Shepherd doth guard with care
    The lambs of the Upper Fold.

The Whole Big Thing—Easter

WALTER B. KNIGHT—1950S

A FATHER AND MOTHER lost three little children in one week by diphtheria. Only the little three-year-old girl escaped. On Easter morning the father, mother, and child were in Sunday School. The father was the superintendent. He led his school in worship and read the Easter message from the Bible without a break in his voice. Many in the school were weeping, but the faces of the father and mother remained serene and calm.

"How can they do it?" men and women asked each other as they left the church.

A fifteen-year-old boy, walking home with his father, said, "Father, I guess the superintendent and his wife *really believe it,* don't they?"

"Believe what?" asked the father.

"The whole, big thing, all of it—EASTER—you know?"

"Of course," answered the father, "all Christians believe it!"

"Not the way they believe it," said the boy, and he began to whistle.

WALTER B. KNIGHT (1897–1995), as a news correspondent in his early years, was ever alert for new stories and illustrations. He wrote his first book when he was fifty, a book of Christian illustrations. He was also a noted preacher.

The Departed Are Still Ours

HENRY WARD BEECHER—MID-NINETEENTH CENTURY

OUR FRIENDS are separated from us because they are lifted higher than our faculties can go. Our child dies. It is the last we can see of him here. He is lifted so far above us we cannot follow him. He was our child; he was cradled in our arms; he clambered upon our knees. But instantly in the twinkling of an eye, God took him, and lifted him up into his own sphere. And we see him not. But it is because we are not yet developed enough. We cannot see things spiritual with carnal eyes. But they who have walked with us here, who have gone beyond us, and whom we cannot see, are still ours. They are more ours than they ever were before. We cannot commune with them as we once could because they are infinitely lifted above those conditions in which we are able to commune. We remain here and are subject to the laws of this realm. They have gone where they speak a higher language, and live in a higher sphere. But this silence is not the silence of vacuity, and this mystery is not the mystery of darkness and death. Theirs is the glory; ours is waiting for it. Theirs is the realization; ours is the hoping for it. Theirs is the perfection; ours is the immaturity striving to be ripe. And when the day comes that we shall disappear from these earthly scenes, we shall be joined to them again; not as we were—for we shall not then be as we were—but as they are, with God. We shall be like them and Him.

They who have walked with us here, who have gone beyond us, and whom we cannot see, are still ours.

Henry Ward Beecher (1813–1887) was the son of well-known preacher Lyman Beecher and brother of the novelist Harriet Beecher Stowe. After serving eight years as pastor of the Second Presbyterian Church in Indianapolis, Indiana, he was called to the Plymouth Congregational Church, Brooklyn, New York, where he remained till his death forty years later. Beecher was judged one of the outstanding preachers of his generation.

CHAPTER 7

Hosts of Heaven

A Scene in Heaven: God Explains His Plan

JOHN MILTON—1671

But [Satan had unwittingly] fulfilled
The purposed counsel pre-ordained and fixed
Of the Most High, who, in full frequence bright
Of angels, thus to Gabriel smiling spake:
"Gabriel, this day by proof thou shalt behold,
Thou and all angels conversant on earth
With man or men's affairs, how I begin
To verify that solemn message, late
On which I sent thee to the virgin pure
In Galilee, that she should bear a Son
Great in renown, and called the Son of God;
Then told'st her, doubting how these things could be
To her a virgin, that on her should come
The Holy Ghost, and the power of the Highest
O'ershadow her: this man, born and now up-grown,
To show him worthy of his birth divine
And high prediction, henceforth I expose
To Satan; let him tempt and now assay
His utmost subtlety, because he boasts
And vaunts of his great cunning to the throng
Of his apostasy: he might have learned
Less overweening, since he failed in Job,

Whose constant perseverance overcame
Whate'er his cruel malice could invent.
He now shall know I can produce a man
Of female seed, far abler to resist
All his solicitations, and at length
All his vast force, and drive him back to Hell,
Winning by conquest what the first man lost
By fallacy surprised. But first I mean
To exercise him in the wilderness;
There he shall first lay down the rudiments
Of his great warfare, ere I send him forth
To conquer Sin and Death, the two grand foes,
By humiliation and strong sufferance:
His weakness shall o'ercome Satanic strength,
And all the world, and mass of sinful flesh;
That all the angels and ethereal powers,
They now, and men hereafter, may discern,
From what consummate virtue I have chose
This perfect man, by merit called my Son,
To earn salvation for the sons of men."

So spake the eternal Father, and all Heaven
Admiring stood a space; then into hymns
Burst forth, and in celestial measures moved,
Circling the throne and singing, while the hand
Sung with the voice; and this the argument:

"Victory and triumph to the Son of God
Now entering his great duel, not of arms,
But to vanquish by wisdom hellish wiles.
The father knows the Son; therefore secure
Ventures his filial virtue, though untried,
Against whate'er may tempt, whate'er seduce,
Allure, or terrify, or undermine.
Be frustrate, all ye stratagems of Hell,
And devilish machinations come to nought."

So they in Heaven their odes and vigils tuned.

John Milton (1608–1674), English poet and author of controversial theological books, was associated with the Puritan movement though an independent thinker. He became blind in 1651, but this failed to restrain his creative output. His most famous work, *Paradise Lost,* of 1667, was followed four years later by *Paradise Regained.* Milton is regarded as one of the most powerful and eloquent poets of the English language.

God's Entourage

John Gilmore—1989

Angels were more God's entourage than heaven's inhabitants. His immensity is partly conveyed by the myriad attendants and angels at his beck. Angels carried out God's orders. Their function was to "do service in the wings." Because their service was not frivolous, but vital, we are not to think of them as ethereal ornaments that hung around to look pretty. They wait on Jesus, not because he is helpless or unwilling to work, but to show his greatness and carry out his will.

Angels are frequently considered fictional figures. Their role in Scripture is viewed as similar to the created chorus in an ancient Greek drama. Though they symbolize the Lord's justice in delivering it, they were presented as real beings. In Revelation God gives them specific responsibilities, and sends them on large-scale missions. Global and partial global duties are fulfilled by them. They gave John the visions (see Revelation 22:6). And when John got too impressed with the revealing angel, the angel disclaimed any greatness and exhorted the writer "Worship God!" (22:9).

> *We are not to expect or look for them* [angels] *on earth.*
> *We cannot identify, hear, or see them in life.*

Heaven teems with angels. John wrote, "Again I looked, and I heard angels, thousands and millions of them! They stood around the throne, the four living creatures, and the elders, and sang" praise to Christ

(5:11–12 GNB). Our conversion was described in Hebrews 12:22 as coming "to thousands upon thousands of angels in joyful assembly."

Yet we are not to expect or look for them on earth. We cannot identify, hear, or see them in life. . . . They are meant to serve God and assist those searching for him (see Hebrews 1:14). . . .

Do angels retrieve the saints from the earth in death and at his second coming? When martyr Stephen died, he saw Jesus stand to receive him (see Acts 7:56). He then prayed, "Lord Jesus, receive my spirit" (Acts 7:59). Jesus' earlier promise, to "receive you unto myself" (John 14:3 KJV) may mean that Jesus himself actually fetches, as well as greets, his dying saints, not only at his second coming, but also in their deaths.

JOHN GILMORE, a graduate of Denver Seminary, is a researcher and author of books written especially for seniors.

Worshiping the Holy God

STEVEN J. LAWSON—1995

WORSHIP INVOLVES a declaration of His greatness. Here is the worship by the angels, as recorded by John, in which the host of Heaven declare the greatness of God.

> *The four living creatures, each one of them having six wings, are full of eyes around and within; and day and night they do not cease to say,* "HOLY, HOLY, HOLY, *is* THE LORD GOD, THE ALMIGHTY, WHO WAS AND WHO IS AND WHO IS TO COME." *(Revelation 4:8 NASB)*

These heavenly creatures—literally, "living ones"—are angelic beings. According to Ezekiel 10:20, these are the cherubim—angelic attendants around God's throne who serve as guardians of His holiness, composing the highest order of the angelic population.

What are these cherubim doing? They are doing what they were created to do—they are worshiping the living God. They offer incessant praise, continuous worship, and unending tribute to God. Certainly this does not preclude other heavenly duties and cosmic functions. While worship is not their sole activity, it is their chief priority.

These angelic worshipers in Heaven adore God first for His holiness. Day and night the heavenly host is crying out "HOLY, HOLY, HOLY" (Revelation 4:8). . . .

With intentional repetition, the angels echo this ascription of greatness three times—*holy, holy, holy.* This means that God is holy to the supreme or superlative degree. . . . He is the holiest Being in all the universe. . . .

The angels are also praising God for *His sovereignty.* This One who is holy is none other than "THE LORD GOD" (Revelation 4:8).

Lord is the key word here. . . . As the Lord God, He alone possesses the right to rule. His throne is the highest authority. His will is unrivaled and supreme. He has the authority to do *whatever* He pleases, *whenever* He pleases, with *whomever* He pleases. . . . He has absolute control over all of His creation. . . .

Further, the angels in Heaven are praising God for *His Omnipotence.* He is declared to be "THE ALMIGHTY" (Revelation 4:8). This means that He is all-powerful. . . . His power knows no limits. He uses His power to accomplish His perfect will with absolute ease. . . .

God is praised by the angels for *His eternality.* He is "THE LORD GOD who was and who is and who is to come" (Revelation 4:8). God is eternal. There has never been a time in the past when God was not. There will never be a time in the future when God will not be. . . .

The Psalmist writes, "Even from everlasting to everlasting, Thou art God" (Psalm 90:2 KJV). That's God—from eternity past to eternity future. . . .

The angels are praising God because of *His self-existence.* As the God "who is," He depends on nothing outside of Himself to exist. He needs nothing outside of Himself to be Himself. He is totally complete within Himself. . . .

Finally, the angels are praising God for *His immutability.* He is "THE LORD GOD who was and who is and who is to come" (Revelation 4:8). . . .

Every aspect about God is unchanging. He is changeless in His character. Changeless in His will. Changeless in His Word. God never changes.

STEVEN J. LAWSON was the senior pastor of Dauphin Way Baptist Church in Mobile, Alabama, and is the author of eight popular books and numerous articles. Dr. Lawson serves on the board for The Master's Seminary and is a Ministerial Advisory Board member for Reformed Theological Seminary.

The Saintly Host

DANTE ALIGHIERI — 1306–1321

In fashion then as of a snow-white rose
Displayed itself to me the saintly host,
Whom Christ in his own blood had made his bride,
But the other host, that flying sees and sings
The glory of Him who doth enamour it,
And the goodness that created it so noble,
Even as a swarm of bees, that sinks in flowers
One moment, and the next returns again
To where its labour is to sweetness turned,
Sank into the great flower, that is adorned
With leaves so many, and thence reascended
To where its love abideth evermore.
Their faces had they all of living flame,
And wings of gold, and all the rest so white
No snow unto that limit doth attain.
From bench to bench, into the flower descending,
They carried something of the peace and ardour
Which by the fanning of their flanks they won.
Nor did the interposing 'twixt the flower
And what was o'er it of such plenitude
Of flying shapes impede the sight and splendour;
Because the light divine so penetrates
The universe, according to its merit,
That naught can be an obstacle against it.

This realm secure and full of gladsomeness,
 Crowded with ancient people and with modern,
 Unto one mark had all its look and love.
O Trinal Light, that in a single star
 Sparkling upon their sight so satisfies them,
 Look down upon our tempest here below!

DANTE ALIGHIERI (1265–1321), growing up in the Italian city-state of Florence, fell in love with a girl named Beatrice whom he idolized but never really met. Though Beatrice died young, she remained the inspiration for Dante's poetry. Exiled from Florence because of his support for a losing faction, he wandered through several Italian cities and finally settled in Ravenna. He spent his later years completing his great work, *The Divine Comedy,* which culminates in a vision of Paradise.

The Continuing Landscape of Faith

KEN GIRE—2006

I HAVE HAD MOMENTS when it seemed I was at the railing that separates heaven and earth, and there was offered a sacrament. The sacrament may have been some hauntingly beautiful music or the echo of an elk bugling in the mountains. It may have been a freshly-cut-peach sunset or a crayoned work of refrigerator art. It may have been a verse of Scripture or a line from Shakespeare. Whatever it was, I sensed that something sacred was being offered me. Receiving it, I knew somehow, and with great certainty, that this was not my home, that my home was the place of my deepest longings, somewhere beyond the fields we know, somewhere that is beautiful beyond telling.

Someday not only will we become beautiful, the whole creation will become beautiful (see Romans 8:18–22). *Stunningly* beautiful. For eye has not seen, nor ear heard, nor mind imagined all that God has prepared for those who love Him (see 1 Corinthians 2:9). The beauty of the most breathtaking mountains here is but a shadow of what awaits us there.

Ken Gire is the author of more than a dozen books and winner of two God Medallion awards and two C.S. Lewis Honor Book awards. He is a full-time writer and speaker. Ken has been involved in the ministries of Young Life and Insight for Living. He is a graduate of Texas Christian University and Dallas Theological Seminary.

You Only Die Once

Margie Little Jenkins—2002

There are many things I don't understand about the nature of life and death; it is truly God's mystery. Believing that God is in charge of the world and all that is in it may take a leap of faith, but Mom and Dad gave me the gift of trusting in a loving God. I learned to believe that I was loved by my parents and my God.

Heaven is like that: a mystery that is beyond my understanding. I know that God is good and wants the best for all of us. He is eternal, and He will always be our guide, if we are willing to follow and trust Him. He promises us a heaven where all our questions will be answered, where we will be free of pain, and where we will be joined with other believers in love and happiness. I believe that heaven will be so glorious that we cannot even imagine the peace and joy that is in store for us. A grand reunion awaits me when Mom and Dad and my God welcome me with open arms into my life after death.

Margie Little Jenkins is a longtime, highly regarded Houston therapist who has counseled numerous cancer patients and other terminally ill clients and conducted in-depth end-of-life seminars. She also spent many hours helping her own father—who lived to be a hundred—prepare to leave his family home of sixty-five years and move to a nursing home.

The Shining Ones

John Bunyan—1678

Now I further saw, that betwixt them and the gate was a river; but there was no bridge to go over, and the river was very deep. At the sight, therefore, of this river, the pilgrims were much stunned; but the men that went with them said, "You must go through, or you cannot come at the gate." . . .

Now, upon the bank of the river, on the other side, they saw the two Shining Men again, who there waited for them. Wherefore, being come out of the river, they saluted them, saying, "We are ministering spirits, sent forth to minister for those that shall be heirs of salvation." Thus they went along towards the gate. Now, you must note that the City stood upon a mighty hill; but the pilgrims went up that hill with ease, because they had these two men to lead them up by the arms; also they had left their mortal garments behind them in the river; for though they went in with them, they came out without them. They therefore went up here with much agility and speed though the foundation upon which the City was framed was higher than the clouds. They therefore went up through the regions of the air, sweetly talking as they went, being comforted because they had safely got over the river, and had such glorious companions to attend them.

The talk they had with the Shining Ones, was about the glory of the place; who told them that the beauty and glory of it were inexpressible. "There," said they, "is the Mount Zion, the heavenly Jerusalem, the innumerable company of angels, and the spirits of just men made perfect. You are going now," said they, "to the Paradise of God, wherein you shall see the tree of life, and eat of the never-fading fruits thereof; and when you come there, you shall have white robes given you, and your walk and talk shall be every day with the King, even all the days of eternity. There you shall not see again such things as you saw when you were in the lower region upon earth; to wit, sorrow, sickness, affliction, and death; 'for the former things are passed away.' You are going now to Abraham, to Isaac, and Jacob, and to the prophets, men that God hath taken away from the evil to come, and that are now resting upon their beds, each one walking in his righteousness." The men then asked, "What must we do in the holy place?" To whom it was answered, "You must there receive the comfort of all your toil, and have joy for all your sorrow; you must reap what you have sown, even the fruit of all your prayers, and tears, and sufferings for the King by the way. In that place you must wear crowns of gold, and enjoy the perpetual sight and visions of the Holy One; for there you shall see Him as He is. There also you shall serve Him continually with praise, with shouting and thanksgiving, whom you desired to serve in the world, though with much difficulty, because of the infirmity of your flesh. There your eyes shall be delighted with seeing, and your ears with hearing the pleasant voice of the Mighty One. There you shall enjoy your friends again that are gone thither before you; and there you shall with joy receive even everyone that follows into the holy place after you. There also you shall be clothed with glory and majesty, and put into an equipage fit to ride out with the King of Glory. When He shall come with sound of trumpet in the clouds, as upon the wings of the wind, you shall come with Him; and when He shall sit upon the throne of judgment, you shall sit by Him; yea, and when He shall pass sentence upon all the workers of iniquity, let them be angels or men, you also have a voice in that judgment, because they were His and your enemies. Also, when He shall again return to the City, you shall go, too, with sound of trumpet, and be ever with Him."

Now, while they were thus drawing towards the gate, behold, a company of the heavenly host came out to meet them; to whom it was said by the other two Shining Ones, "These are the men that have loved our Lord when in the world, and that have left all for His holy name; and He hath sent us to fetch them, and we have brought them thus far on their desired journey, that they may go in and look their Redeemer in the face with joy." Then the heavenly host gave a great shout, saying, "Blessed are they which are called to the marriage supper of the Lamb." There came out also at this time to meet them several of the King's trumpeters, clothed in white and shining raiment, who, with melodious noises and loud, made even the heavens to echo with their sound. These trumpeters saluted Christian and his fellow with ten thousand welcomes from the world; and this they did with shouting and sound of trumpet.

This done, they compassed them round on every side; some went before, some behind, and some on the right hand, some on the left (as it were to guard them through the upper regions), continually sounding as they went, with melodious noise, in notes on high: so that the very sight was to them that could behold it as if heaven itself was come down to meet them. Thus, therefore, they walked on together; and, as they walked, ever and anon these trumpeters, even with joyful sound, would, by mixing their music with looks and gestures, still signify to Christian and his brother how welcome they were into their company, and with what gladness they came to meet them. And now were these two men as it were in heaven, before they came at it, being swallowed up with the sight of angels, and with hearing of their melodious notes. Here also they had the City itself in view, and they thought they heard all the bells therein to ring, and welcome them thereto. But, above all, the warm and joyful thoughts that they had about their own dwelling there with such company, and that for ever and ever, oh! by what tongue or pen can their glorious joy be expressed?

And thus they came up to the gate. . . .

Now, I saw in my dream that these two men went in at the gate; and lo! as they entered, they were transfigured; and they had raiment put on that shone like gold. There were also that met them with harps and crowns, and gave them to them—the harps to praise withal, and the crowns in token of honor. Then I heard in my dream, that all the bells in the City rang again for joy, and that it was said unto them, "Enter ye into the joy of your Lord." I also heard the men themselves, that they sang with a loud voice, saying, "Blessing, and honor, and glory, and power, be unto Him that sitteth upon the throne, and unto the Lamb, forever and ever!"

Now, just as the gates were opened to let in the men, I looked in after them, and behold, the City shone like the sun; the streets also were paved with gold; and in them walked many men with crowns on their heads, palms in their hands, and golden harps to sing praises withal.

There were also of them that had wings, and they answered one another without intermission, saying, "Holy, holy, holy is the Lord!" And, after that, they shut up the gates; which when I had seen, I wished myself among them.

For biographical information on this author, see page 36.

How Will We Relate to Angels?

JONI EARECKSON TADA—1995

THE MORE HEAVENLY MINDED I become, the more convinced I am of the presence of angels in my life, whether it's acknowledging their whereabouts in a sports arena or calling them forth to surround the bedside of someone who is sick. Their job description has included bringing messages, as they did to the seven churches in the book of Revelation. . . .

If angels rejoiced so happily over our conversion, how much more will they rejoice over us when we arrive at the foot of God's throne.

One of the best parts of heaven may be getting to know and fellowshiping with angels. They love God and they enjoy us. In a parable about sinners gaining entrance into the kingdom of heaven, Jesus said, "I tell you, there is rejoicing in the presence of the angels of God over one sinner who repents" (Luke 15:10). If angels rejoiced so happily over our conversion, how much more will they rejoice over us when we arrive at the foot of God's throne. To the angels, we will be a source of eternal joy. They will see our redemption completed. From beginning to end. . . .

We will also worship with the angels. They've had a lot of practice at worshiping, as well as access to heaven's throne. They've seen it all. Yet when we arrive in heaven, it will be their privilege to worship with us. Just think what our worship will sound like. In Revelation 5:11–13, angels crowd before the throne, "numbering thousands upon thousands, and ten thousand times ten thousand. . . . In a loud voice they sang: 'Worthy is the Lamb, who was slain, to receive power and wealth and wisdom and strength and honor and glory and praise!'". . .

Angels will also serve us in heaven. Their job description in Hebrews 1:14 extends beyond just earth. Angels will be subject to us in eternity. We will reign with Jesus; and if He has been given authority over all the heavenly hosts, then we will reign over angels too. Will we govern a few legions or many? What shall we command them to do in faraway galaxies? How will they aid us on earth to help carry out the kingdom rule? I can't say, but it's thrilling to imagine.

For biographical information on this author, see page 22.

The Glistening Angelic Host

EDMUND SPENSER—1596

Love, lift me up upon thy golden wings
From this base world unto thy heaven's height,
Where I may see those admirable things
Which there thou workest by thy sovereign might,
Far above feeble reach of earthly sight,
That I thereof an heavenly hymn may sing
Unto the God of Love, high heaven's king. . . .

Yet, O most blessed Spirit! pure lamp of light,
Eternal spring of grace and wisdom true,
Vouchsafe to shed into my barren sprite
Some little drop of thy celestial dew,
That may my rhymes with sweet infuse embrue,
And give me words equal unto my thought,
To tell the marvels by thy mercy wrought.

Yet being pregnant still with powerful grace,
And full of fruitful love, that loves to get
Things like himself, and to enlarge his race,
His second brood, though not in power so great,

Yet full of beauty, next He did beget,
An infinite increase of angels bright,
All glist'ning glorious in their Maker's light.

To them the heaven's illimitable height
(Not this round heaven, which we from hence behold,
Adorn'd with thousand lamps of burning light,
And with ten thousand gems of shining gold,)
He gave as their inheritance to hold,
That they might serve Him in eternal bliss,
And be partakers of those joys of His.

There they in their trinal triplicities
About Him wait, and on His will depend,
Either with nimble wings to cut the skies,
When He them on His messages doth send,
Or on his own dread presence to attend,
Where they behold the glory of His light,
And carol hymns of love both day and night.

Both day, and night, is unto them all one;
For He His beams doth still unto them extend,
That darkness there appeareth never none;
Ne hath their day, ne hath their bliss, an end,
But there their termless time in pleasure spend;
Ne ever should their happiness decay,
Had not they dared their Lord to disobey.

Edmund Spenser (1552–1599) was born in London and received an education in the classics. In 1580 he was appointed secretary to the Lord Deputy of Ireland, then being colonized by the English. He lived there during most of the rest of his life, but due to uprisings against English rule, he returned to London shortly before his death. Although *The Faerie Queene* is considered Spenser's masterpiece, some of his other poetry is more widely read today. Spenser was buried in Westminster Abbey, his tomb next to that of Chaucer.

Who Are the Angels?

LARRY LIBBY—1993

ANGELS ARE GOD'S LETTER CARRIERS. Well, yes, I'm sure they do more than that. The Bible says they are spirits who serve God and are sent to help those who love Jesus.

But time after time God has sent His angels through Heaven's door to carry important messages to Earth. How God loves the world! How much He wants to communicate with the people He created for Himself!

The Bible tells us how God has sent message after message to His people. He has sent important information. He has sent stern warnings. And most of all, He has sent love letters. But how did God's mail get through to people on Earth? Lots of times, by ANGEL EXPRESS.

Most people who have seen angels have been afraid of them. God's letter carriers are swift and powerful and beautiful and so white and shining you can hardly look at them. Fresh from the bright land of Heaven, angels arrive on Earth looking like a flash of lightning in a dark evening sky.

Usually the first thing angels have to tell people is, "Don't be afraid! Don't faint! Don't run away! I'm just an angel with an air mail message from God."

Some of the messages have been very sad. God has told His people the terrible things that would happen because they disobeyed Him. Some of the messages have made people cry and pray hard that God would forgive them and help them.

Other messages have told people what would happen in the far-away future. But the job angels seem to like best (and probably all get in line for) is bringing good news to Earth. Do you remember hearing about the night long ago when Jesus was born? Beneath a star-sprinkled sky, the shepherds were quietly watching over their flocks of sleepy sheep. All at once—

> *An angel of the Lord suddenly stood before them, and the glory of the Lord shone around them, and they were terribly frightened. But the angel said to them, "Do not be afraid. . . . I*

> *bring you good news of great joy. . . . Today in the city of David there has been born for you a Savior who is Christ the Lord" (Luke 2:9–11 NASB).*

That angel had the happy job of bringing absolutely wonderful news. And then it was as if Heaven's door suddenly flew wide open and a million other angels said, "Oh, this is *too much* good news for one angel! We want to deliver the message, too! Let us say the good news, too!" And then all of God's letter carriers seemed to come tumbling out of Heaven in a great excited rush—singing and shouting and praising God and chasing away the darkness of night.

Years and years later, another angel (or maybe it was the same lucky one) got to tell the best news of all.

When Jesus rose from the dead on the very first Easter, that angel put his strong shoulder against the big stone that covered the Lord's tomb. The angel rolled it back and then sat on it! (Do you suppose he sat very straight and stern . . . or sort of smiled and leaned back and crossed his legs?)

He said to two women who were looking for the Lord's dead body, Why are you looking for a living person here? This is a place for the dead. Jesus is not here. He has risen from death! (see Luke 24:5–6).

Angels love to be God's letter carriers. They love being the Angel Express. And God's messages do get delivered, even when Satan wants to stop them.

But tell me, if God loves us so much, why does He use the Angel Express? Why doesn't God leave His beautiful home and deliver the messages to our poor old world Himself? Why doesn't He come to where we live and show us His strong, forever love? He DID, didn't He?

The best and brightest of all God's love letters came special delivery to Bethlehem. The Lord Jesus not only brought the message of love, He was the message of love. He *was* the best Gift God could have ever sent to Earth.

No wonder those angels got so excited!

Larry Libby is an author and editor who has collaborated on writing projects with several bestselling authors and has written articles for well-known Christian magazines.

CHAPTER 8

Treasure in Heaven

Certainty of Our Eternal Reward

CYRIL OF JERUSALEM—*circa 347*

THE REAL AND TRUE LIFE then is the Father, who through the Son in the Holy Spirit pours forth as from a fountain His heavenly gifts to all; and through His love to man, the blessings of the life eternal are promised without fail to us men also. We must not disbelieve the possibility of this, but having an eye not to our own weakness but to His power, we must believe; *for with God all things are possible*. . . .

And many are the proofs concerning the life eternal. And when we desire to gain this eternal life, the sacred Scriptures suggest to us the ways of gaining it; of which, because of the length of our discourse, the texts we now set before you shall be but few, the rest being left to the search of the diligent. They declare at one time that it is by faith; for it is written, *He that believeth on the Son hath eternal life,* and what follows; and again He says Himself, *Verily, verily, I say unto you, He that heareth My word, and believeth Him that sent Me, hath eternal life,* and the rest. . . . But further, it is by departing from evil works, and henceforth serving God; for Paul says, *But now being made free from sin, and become servants to God, ye have your fruit unto sanctification, and the end eternal life.*

And the ways of finding eternal life are many, though I have passed over them by reason of their number. For the Lord in His loving-kindness has opened, not one or two only, but many doors, by which to enter into the life eternal, that, as far as lay in Him, all might enjoy it without hindrance. Thus much have we for the present spoken within compass concerning The Life Eternal, which is the last doctrine of those professed in the Faith, and its termination; which life may we all, both teachers and hearers, by God's grace enjoy!

CYRIL OF JERUSALEM (*circa* 315–386) was bishop of Jerusalem as early as 349. The twenty-four *Catechetical Lectures,* his chief writing that survives, were delivered during Lent and Eastertide to those who were baptized on the Saturday before Easter. They include expositions on the clauses of the Nicene Creed of 325, as in this selection.

An Eternal Inheritance

JOHN F. MACARTHUR—*1996*

OUR INHERITANCE is something entirely different from our rewards. Our eternal inheritance is not merited by works, nor is it apportioned according to them. The apostle Paul ties our inheritance to our adoption as sons. An *inheritance* by definition is not a reward for merit earned. It is a birthright.

Furthermore, there was a significant difference between Roman law and Jewish custom on the matter of a child's inheritance. By Jewish law, the eldest son always received a double portion of the inheritance. Under the Roman system, all children could receive equal shares. When Paul wrote, "if children, then . . . joint-heirs with Christ" (Romans 8:17 KJV), he was addressing a Roman audience. The context indicates his emphasis was on the equality of God's children and the security of every Christian's inheritance.

Writing to the Galatians, Paul made a similar point: "And *if ye be Christ's,* then are ye Abraham's seed, and heirs according to the promise" (Galatians 3:29 KJV, emphasis added). He echoed the thought a chapter later: "And *because ye are sons,* God hath sent forth the Spirit of his Son into your hearts, crying, Abba, Father. Wherefore thou art no more a servant, but a son; and if a son, then an heir of God through

Christ" (4:6–7 KJV, emphasis added). The inheritance is not a reward for a faithful servant (as were the rewards in most of Jesus' parables). It is a birthright for every child of the Father.

Plainly, Scripture is teaching that all Christians will receive a full share of the inheritance of heaven. *Every* believer will "inherit all things" (Revelation 21:7 KJV), so the inheritance isn't carved up and apportioned on the basis of worthiness. And when God says, "I will be his God, and he shall be my son"—He is saying that heaven will be not only our dwelling-place, but also our possession. We will be there not as boarders, but as full-fledged members of the family. What an inexpressible privilege that is!

For biographical information on this author, see page 25.

We Sing of That Land

FANNY J. CROSBY—1892

We sing of a land where the servants of God
Shall meet when their journey is o'er,
And clasp their glad hands as they gather at morn,
To labor and sorrow no more.

We sing of a land where the leaves never fall,
A land where their bloom never dies;
And Jesus Himself, with his own loving hand,
Will wipe ev'ry tear from our eyes.

We sing of the palms that the conquerors wave,
Who triumphed through Jesus our Lord;
Who fought to the last, and with shouts on their tongues
Went home to receive their reward.

We sing of the friends who are waiting to-day
For us in that region so fair;

But who can describe what a joy it will be
To know that indeed we are there?

We sing of the beautiful mansions of rest
Our Savior has gone to prepare,
And oh, when we think of the bliss they unfold,
In spirit, how oft we are there.

For biographical information on this author, see page 63.

Rewarded by His Generosity

Erwin W. Lutzer—1998

I passionately agree that when we put our faith in Christ we are declared righteous by God because of Christ and not because of our works. Our deeds before our conversion are of no merit in the sight of God. "For by grace you have been saved through faith; and that not of yourselves, it is the gift of God; not as a result of works, that no one should boast" (Ephesians 2:8–9 NASB). If anyone . . . thinks that he will be saved because of human effort, he will be tragically disappointed for all of eternity.

> *The works we do after our conversion do not have merit in and of themselves; they have merit only because we are joined to Christ.*

But works done *after* we have received the free gift of eternal life are special to God. Indeed, the same passage (quoted above) that affirms we are saved by faith alone because of grace continues: "For we are His workmanship, created in Christ Jesus for good works, which God prepared beforehand that we should walk in them" (v. 10 NASB). These works are sought by God and honor Him. We should strive to please Him, and for such works we shall be rewarded. Although we shy away from thinking that something we do has merit, Christ did not hesitate to promise that those who performed sacrificial acts would be "repaid" (Luke 14:14 NASB). . . .

Of course, the works we do after our conversion do not have merit in and of themselves; they have merit only because we are joined to Christ. He takes our imperfect works and makes them acceptable to the Father. Also, we should not think that God must pay us like an employer who has a legal obligation to pay his employee. As we shall learn later, our good deeds are done only because God gives us the desire and ability to do them. They are a gift of His grace to us. Furthermore, no child is expected to work for his inheritance; indeed, it is not possible that he could "earn" all that the Father is pleased to give him.

But—and this must be stressed—the father *tests* his son to prove him worthy; the father uses that which is least to see if his child can be trusted with a greater share of the inheritance. *Dependability on earth translates into greater responsibility in heaven.* Just so, Christ will judge us on the basis of our worthiness, and thus our present faithfulness or lack thereof will have eternal, heavenly repercussions! . . .

This does not mean that rewards are based on a day's pay for a day's work. God will reward us out of proportion to the work we have done. Though it appears that He would have no reason to reward us, He has placed Himself under a loving obligation to do so. If He didn't reward us, the author of Hebrews says, He would be "unjust." "For God is not unjust so as to forget your work and the love which you have shown toward His name, in having ministered and in still ministering to the saints" (Hebrews 6:10 NASB).

When we consider that the ultimate reward is to rule with Christ as a joint-heir, charged with the responsibility of authority over all God's possessions, it is clear that rewards are never earned in the usual sense of the word. God has obligated Himself to give us rewards, but this is strictly because of His grace. We can demand nothing; indeed, after we have done our best we are still unworthy servants, having "done only that which we ought to have done" (Luke 17:10 NASB). God has chosen to give us what we have no right to either demand or expect. *We are rewarded because of His generosity, not His obligation.*

Chapter 8

Erwin W. Lutzer is the senior pastor of Moody Church in Chicago, as well as a sought-after speaker at leadership and church conferences. He is the author of numerous books.

Comforts in Heaven

J. C. Ryle — mid-nineteenth century

But reader, there are positive things told us about the glory yet to come upon the heirs of God, which ought not to be kept back. There are many sweet, pleasant, and unspeakable comforts in their future inheritance, which all true Christians would do well to consider. There are cordials for fainting pilgrims in many words and expressions of Scripture, which you and I ought to lay up against time of need.

Is *knowledge* pleasant to us now? Is the little that we know of God, and Christ, and in the Bible, precious to our souls, and do we long for more? We shall have it perfectly in glory. What says the Scripture?—"Then shall I know even as also I am known" (1 Corinthians 13:12 KJV). Blessed be God, there will be no more disagreements among believers! Episcopalians and Presbyterians, Calvinists and Arminians, Millenarians and Anti-Millenarians, friends of Establishments and friends of the Voluntary system, advocates of infant baptism and advocates of adult baptism,—all will at length be of one mind. The former ignorance will have passed away. We shall marvel to find how childish and blind we have been.

Is *holiness* pleasant to us now? Is sin the burden and bitterness of our lives? Do we long for entire conformity to the image of God? We shall have it perfectly in glory. What says the Scripture?—Christ gave Himself for the Church, "that he might present it to himself a glorious church, not having spot or wrinkle, or any such thing" (Ephesians 5:27 KJV). Oh, the blessedness of an eternal good-bye to sin! Oh, how little the best of us do at present! Oh, what unutterable corruption sticks, like birdlime, to all our motives, all our thoughts, all our words, all our actions! Oh, how many of us, like Naphtali, are godly in our words, but, like Reuben, unstable in our works! Thank God, all this shall be changed!

Is *rest* pleasant to us now? Do we often feel faint though pursuing? Do we long for a world in which we need not be always watching and warring? We shall have it perfectly in glory. What saith the Scripture?— "There remaineth therefore a rest for the people of God" (Hebrews 4:9 KJV). The daily, hourly conflict with the world, the flesh, and the devil, shall at length be at an end: the enemy shall be bound; the warfare shall be over; the wicked shall at last cease from troubling; the weary shall at length be at rest. There shall be a great calm.

Is *service* pleasant to us now? Do we find it sweet to work for Christ, and yet groan, being burdened by a feeble body? Is our spirit often willing, but hampered and clogged by the poor weak flesh? Have our hearts burned within us when we have been allowed to give a cup of cold water for Christ's sake; and have we sighed to think what unprofitable servants we are? Let us take comfort. We shall be able to serve perfectly in glory, and without weariness. What saith the Scripture?—they "serve him day and night in his temple" (Revelation 7:15 KJV).

Is *satisfaction* pleasant to us now? Do we find the world empty? Do we long for the filling up of every void place and gap in our hearts? We shall have it perfectly in glory. We shall no longer have to mourn over cracks in all our earthen vessels, and thorns in all our roses, and bitter dregs in all our sweet cups. We shall no longer lament, with Jonah, over withered gourds. We shall no longer say, with Solomon, "All is vanity and vexation of spirit." We shall no longer cry, with aged David, "I have seen an end of all perfection." What saith the Scripture?—"I shall be satisfied, when I awake, with thy likeness" (Psalm 17:15 KJV).

Is *communion with the saints* pleasant to us now? Do we feel that we are never so happy as when we are with the excellent of the earth? Are we never so much at home as in their company? We shall have it perfectly in glory. What saith the Scripture?—"The Son of man shall send forth his angels, and they shall gather out of his kingdom all things that offend, and them which do iniquity." "He shall send his angels with a great sound of a trumpet; and they shall gather together his elect from the four winds" (Matthew 13:41; 24:31 KJV). Praised be God, we shall see all the saints of whom we have read in the Bible, and in whose steps we have tried to walk. . . .

Is *communion with Christ* pleasant to us now? Do we find His name precious to us? Do we feel our hearts burn within us at the thought of His dying love? We shall have perfect communion with Him in glory. "So shall we ever be with the Lord" (1 Thessalonians 4:17 KJV). We shall be with Him in paradise: we shall see His face in the kingdom. These eyes of ours will behold those hands and feet which were pierced with nails, and that head which was crowned with thorns. Where He is, there will the sons of God be. When He comes, they will come with Him: when He sits down in His glory, they shall sit down by His side. Blessed prospects indeed! I am a dying man in a dying world; all before me is unseen: the world to come is a harbour unknown! But Christ is there, and that is enough. Surely if there is rest and peace in following Him by faith on earth, there will be far more rest and peace when you see Him face to face. If we have found it good to follow the pillar of cloud and fire in the wilderness, we shall find it a thousand times better to sit down in our eternal inheritance with our Joshua, in the promised land.

JOHN C. RYLE (1816–1900), son of a banker in Cheshire County, England, attended Eton and then Oxford. In 1841 he was ordained a minister in the Church of England. After serving in several parishes, in 1880 he was consecrated bishop of Liverpool. Bishop Ryle became known as a defender of the evangelical Reformed faith as expressed in the Thirty-nine Articles of Religion of the Church of England, and he was a prolific writer.

A Special Crown for Each One

JOHN CALVIN—1559

IF OUR LORD will share his glory, power, and righteousness with the elect, nay, will give himself to be enjoyed by them; and what is better still, will, in a manner, become one with them, let us remember that every kind of happiness is herein included. But when we have made great progress in thus meditating, let us understand that if the conceptions of our minds be contrasted with the sublimity of the mystery, we are still halting at the very entrance. The more necessary is it for us to cultivate sobriety in this matter, lest, unmindful of our feeble capacity, we presume to take too lofty a flight, and be overwhelmed by the brightness of the celestial glory. We feel how much we are stimulated by an excessive desire of knowing more than is given us to know, and hence frivolous and noxious questions are ever and anon springing forth: by frivolous, I mean questions from which no advantage can be extracted. But there is a second class which is worse than frivolous; because those who indulge in them involve themselves in hurtful speculations. Hence I call them noxious. The doctrine of Scripture on the subject ought not to be made the ground of any controversy, and it is that as God, in the varied distribution of gifts to his saints in this world, gives them unequal degrees of light, so when he shall crown his gifts, their degrees of glory in heaven will also be unequal. When Paul says, "Ye are our glory and joy" (1 Thessalonians 2:20 KJV), his words do not apply indiscriminately to all; nor do those of our Saviour to his apostles, "Ye also shall sit upon twelve thrones, judging the twelve tribes of Israel" (Matthew 19:28 KJV). But Paul, who knew that as God enriches the saints with spiritual gifts in this world, he will in like manner adorn them with glory in heaven, hesitates not to say, that a special crown is laid up for him in proportion to his labors. Our Saviour, also, to commend the dignity of the office which he had conferred on the apostles, reminds them that the fruit of it is laid up in heaven. This, too, Daniel says, "They that be wise shall shine as the brightness of the firmament; and they that turn many to righteousness as the stars for ever and ever" (Daniel 12:3 KJV). Any one who attentively considers the Scriptures will see not only that they promise eternal life to believers, but a special reward to each. Hence the expression of Paul, "The Lord grant unto him that he may find mercy of the Lord in that day" (2 Timothy 1:18 KJV). This is confirmed by our Saviour's promise, that they "shall receive an hundredfold, and shall inherit everlasting life" (Matthew 19:29 KJV). In short, as Christ, by the manifold variety of his gifts, begins the glory of his body in this world, and gradually increases it, so he will complete it in heaven.

JOHN CALVIN (1509–1564), or JEAN CAUVIN, studied theology in Paris but came under Protestant influence. He fled to Switzerland to escape persecution by the French monarch. He planned a life as a scholar, but instead became organizer of the Reformation in Geneva. His administration of both church and city life was based on strict biblical precepts. The *Institutes of the Christian Religion* is his most important writing. Its final version appeared in Latin in 1559 and in French the following year, and it has been a standard authority for Reformed Protestant theology since that time.

The Chalice of Heavenly Wisdom

BERNARD OF CLAIRVAUX—TWELFTH CENTURY

WHAT OF THE SOULS already released from their bodies? We believe that they are overwhelmed in that vast sea of eternal light and of luminous eternity. But no one denies that they still hope and desire to receive their bodies again: whence it is plain that they are not yet wholly transformed, and that something of self remains yet unsurrendered. Not until death is swallowed up in victory, and perennial light overflows the uttermost bounds of darkness, not until celestial glory clothes our bodies, can our souls be freed entirely from self and give themselves up to God. For until then souls are bound to bodies, if not by a vital connection of sense, still by natural affection; so that without their bodies they cannot attain to their perfect consummation, nor would they if they could. And although there is no defect in the soul itself before the restoration of its body, since it has already attained to the highest state of which it is by itself capable, yet the spirit would not yearn for reunion with the flesh if without the flesh it could be consummated.

Illness is an aid to penitence; death is the gate of rest; and the resurrection will bring consummation.

And finally, "Precious in the sight of the Lord is the death of His saints" (Psalm 116:15 KJV). But if their death is precious, what must such a life as theirs be! No wonder that the body shall seem to add fresh glory to the spirit; for though it is weak and mortal, it has availed not a little for mutual help. How truly he spake who said, "All things work together for good to them that love God" (Romans 8:28 KJV). The body is a help to the soul that loves God, even when it is ill, even when it is dead, and all the more when it is raised again from the dead: for illness is an aid to penitence; death is the gate of rest; and the resurrection will bring consummation. So, rightly, the soul would not be perfected without the body, since she recognizes that in every condition it has been needful to her good. . . .

At first then the faithful soul eats her bread, but alas! in the sweat of her face. Dwelling in the flesh, she walks as yet by faith, which must work through love. As faith without [works] is dead, so work itself is food for her; even as our Lord saith, "My meat is to do the will of him that sent me" (John 4:34). When the flesh is laid aside, she eats no more the bread of carefulness, but is allowed to drink deeply of the wine of love, as if after a repast. . . . At last she attains to that chalice of the heavenly wisdom, of which it is written, "My cup shall be full." Now indeed she is refreshed with the abundance of the house of God, where all selfish, carking [i.e., annoying—ed.] care is done away, and where, for ever safe, she drinks the fruit of the vine, new and pure, with Christ in the Kingdom of His Father (see Matthew 26:29).

It is Wisdom who spreads this threefold supper where all the repast is love; Wisdom who feeds the toilers, who gives drink to those who rest, who floods with rapture those that reign with Christ. Even as at an earthly banquet custom and nature serve meat first and then wine, so here. Before death, while we are still in mortal flesh, we eat the labors of our hands, we swallow with an effort the food so gained; but after death, we shall begin eagerly to drink in the spiritual life and finally, reunited to our bodies, and rejoicing in fullness of delight, we shall be refreshed with immortality. This is what the Bridegroom means when He saith: "Eat, O friends; drink, yea, drink abundantly, O beloved." Eat before death; begin to drink after death; drink abundantly after the resurrection. Rightly are they called beloved who have drunk abundantly of love; rightly do they drink abundantly who are worthy to be brought to the marriage supper of the Lamb, eating and drinking at His table in His Kingdom (see Revelation 19:9; Luke 22:30). At that supper, He shall present to Himself a glorious Church, not having spot, or wrinkle, or any such thing (see Ephesians 5:27). Then truly shall He refresh His beloved; then He shall give them drink of His pleasures, as out of the river (see Psalm 36:8). While the Bridegroom clasps the Bride in tender, pure embrace, then the rivers of the flood thereof shall make glad the city of God (see Psalm 46:4). And this refers to the Son of God Himself, who will come forth and serve them, even as He hath promised; so that in that day the righteous shall be glad and rejoice before God: they shall also be merry and joyful (see Psalm 68:3). Here indeed is appeasement without weariness: here never-quenched thirst for knowledge, without distress; here eternal and infinite desire which knows no want; here, finally, is that sober inebriation which comes not from drinking new wine but from enjoying God (see Acts 2:13).

Bernard of Clairvaux (1090–1153), after becoming a monk, was asked to establish a new monastery and chose Clairvaux, in the Champagne region of France, as its location. He and his order, the Cistercians, soon became powerful forces in the spiritual life of Europe. It was his austere but gracious character, rather than his intellect, that gave Bernard his influence, and in his writings he focused on the simple and pure love of God.

Is Suffering Worth It?

Joni Eareckson Tada and Steven Estes—1997

Is all the bleeding worth the benefit?

More than we realize. "For our light and momentary troubles are achieving for us an eternal glory that far outweighs them all" (2 Corinthians 4:17). Heaven knows its pleasures and joys, the ecstasy and elation. As far as heaven is concerned, our troubles are "light" in comparison. This is another verse written in end-time perspective, telling us, "This is the way it will all turn out, this is the way it will be, you'll see!" Again, it's a matter of faith. A pile of problems are on one side of the scale; heaven's glory, the other.

If the problem-side of the scale seems heavy, then focus your faith on the glory-side. When you do, you're a Rumpelstiltskin weaving straw into gold; like a divine spinning wheel, your affliction "*worketh* . . . a far more exceeding and eternal weight of glory" (2 Corinthians 4:17 KJV). It's as J. B. Phillips paraphrases, "These little troubles (which are really so transitory) are winning for us a permanent, glorious and solid reward out of all proportion to our pain" (2 Corinthians 4:17 PHILLIPS).

It's not merely that heaven will be wonderful *in spite* of our anguish; it will be wonderful *because* of it. Suffering serves us. A faithful response to affliction accrues a *weight* of glory. A bounteous reward. God has every intention of rewarding your endurance. Why else would he meticulously chronicle every one of your tears? "Record my lament; list my tears on your scroll—are they not in your record?" (Psalm 56:8).

Every tear you've cried—think of it—will be redeemed. God will give you indescribable glory for your grief. Not with a general wave of the hand, but in a considered and specific way. Each tear has been listed; each will be recompensed. We know how valuable our tears are in his sight—when Mary anointed Jesus with the valuable perfume, it was her tears with which she washed his feet that moved him most powerfully (see Luke 7:44). The worth of our weeping is underscored again in Revelation 21:4 where "he will wipe every tear from their eyes." It won't be the duty of angels or others. It'll be God's.

"Weeping may endure for a night, but joy cometh in the morning" (Psalm 30:5 KJV).

The more faithful to God we are in the midst of our pain, the more our reward and joy.

Our reward will be our joy. The more faithful to God we are in the midst of our pain, the more our reward and joy. The Gospels are packed with parables of kings honoring servants for their diligence, landlords showering bonuses on faithful laborers, monarchs placing loyal subjects in charge of many cities. Whatever suffering you are going through this minute, your reaction to it affects the eternity you will enjoy. Heaven will be more heavenly to the degree that you have followed Christ on earth. "I consider that our present sufferings are not worth comparing with the glory that will be revealed in us" (Romans 8:18).

It has been said that something so grand, so glorious is going to happen in the world's finale, something so awesome and wonderful—the denouement of the Lord Jesus—that it will suffice for every hurt, it will compensate for every inhumanity, and it will atone for every terror. His glory will fill the universe, and hell will be an afterthought compared to the resplendent brightness of God's cosmos and "the Lamb who gives it light." Heaven's joy far outweighs hell's dread.

For biographical information on these authors, see page 38.

Gifts for the King

RANDY ALCORN—1998

"WELCOME, TRAVELERS," said the girl. "We meet again. You are about to enter the city. Present to us your gifts for the King."

"Gifts?" Malaiki asked.

"Yes. The stones you picked up in the riverbeds."

My heart pounded. I put down my worn sack, just over half-full. Though I'd often tried before, for the first time in the daylight I managed to open it.

I pulled out a stone. It glimmered in the sunlight.

"It's gold!" I said. I reached back into the sack. "Silver! A ruby. Look—two diamonds. An emerald! And this one . . . I've never seen anything like it!"

I was vaguely aware of the others shouting. I looked to see them rifling through their bags, holding up precious stones in the rosy sunlight.

I reached farther into my bag and found what I'd thought were some light stones. I pulled them out and stared at them.

"They're not stones at all," I said. "They're just crumpled balls of straw."

I turned the bag upside down. One last gem fell out, a small one. The rest was straw and stubble.

The girl in black picked up my stones and straw and placed them on a grate connected to a long pole. She held it over the blaze. The fire immediately consumed the straw, while it burned off impurities from the gold and silver and gems. They glowed with an otherworldly beauty, and I stared at them breathlessly, held captive by their radiance.

When I came out of my trance, I turned to Malaiki, now opening her third and final sack. She had dozens of precious gems, perhaps twenty diamonds and chunks of gold and silver. Her eyes danced as she watched the sunlight play on them. The grate was large, and a big warrior affixed it to the pole and held her stones over the fire.

"Well, if that don't beat all!" Gordy said, bouncing around like a child in front of Christmas presents, sucking his teeth and gazing wide-eyed at the precious stones from his two bags. I was amazed at how many stones he'd picked up in such a short time. Gordy had always struck me as being not too quick on the uptake. Yet here he was with three times as many precious stones as I.

So when it comes down to it, who's smart and who's dumb?

For the next hour we all watched Shad go through the rest of his sacks. He stopped to laugh and dance a jig. Then he stood still and solemnly handed each stone, one by one, to the King's envoy. She nodded her approval and put them on a large grate. It took two warriors to help her swing the pole out over the fire. The old man's eye watered as he watched the straw burn away and the precious metals glow in the fire.

I stared at all those stones. How could one old man have carried them all on our journey? In his own strength it would have been impossible—of course, that was it. He'd carried them with the strength of another.

"Thuros, like Earth, is the womb of Charis," whispered a familiar voice beside me. "Choice and consequences. What is done in one world has profound effects on the next."

As I nodded at Marcus, a warrior carrying the fine tools of an artisan stepped forward. He went to the grates where the stones were cooling. He picked up gold and jewels from each grate and masterfully forged them together into crowns of stunning beauty. Then he handed them to my companions, one by one.

"You will cast these at the King's feet," said the girl in black. "And sometimes you will wear them. The King and all the citizens of Charis will be forever reminded of your faithful service. You will remember the meaning of every stone, and so will he. Elyon's book says, 'A scroll of remembrance was written in his presence concerning those who feared the King and honored his name.' All your works are recorded here—every cup of cold water given in his name."

I looked at the stones on my grate, not yet fashioned into a crown. In each of them I saw animated images. I saw in a diamond the moment I first met Gordy in the makeshift jail. I saw in silver the dark, cold day I stood up to David on the mountainside and protected Malaiki. In one very large ruby I saw myself caring for Cliff. But something was very strange—Cliff looked different now. His smoked-glass eyes burned into me, the scars on his hands . . . and feet.

"The Woodman," I said, voice trembling. "Cliff was the Woodman? The King?"

"Yes," Marcus said. "The King is not gone, you know. He walks the planet, disguised as the needy."

I stared at him.

"Do not think it so strange. I sometimes do the same thing myself."

Dumbfounded, I looked back at the other gems. In one I protected Shad from being beaten by the mob that killed Quon. In another, on the perilous ledge of Mount Peirasmos, I told Shaun about the King.

In the other stones I saw many different things, some I'd completely forgotten. Several gems contained images of things done while I was alone, including prayers to the King.

"But no one was even there," I said.

"I was there," said Marcus. "And the King is always there."

"There's no such thing as a private moment," said the girl in black. When I'd heard that before, it had terrified me. Now it thrilled me.

"I have no stones," Victoria said to the messenger, her voice breaking. "Can I not enter the city?"

"Entrance to the city is the King's gift," she said. "He paid your full admission and you accepted his gift. Therefore you may enter freely." She paused and looked at Victoria curiously. "It is sad, though, is it not, that you bring nothing to him?"

"Sad," Victoria mumbled, her eyes drooping. "Yes, very sad."

I remembered then the words spoken by the girl in black when she first told us to pick up stones by night. "In the morning, you will be both glad and sad."

The long night was over, and morning was here at last. I looked at the stones I'd picked up, knowing they were my tribute to the King. Seeing them, I'd never felt so glad.

Then I thought about all the stones within my reach, all those I could have picked up but didn't.

I'd never felt so sad.

For biographical information on this author, see page 34.

Eternity Magnifies Our Joys

THOMAS TRAHERNE — *circa* 1650

THE INFINITY OF GOD is our enjoyment, because it is the region and extent of His dominion. Barely as it comprehends infinite space, it is infinitely delightful; because it is the room and the place of our treasures, the repository of joys, and the dwelling place, yea the seat and throne, and Kingdom of our souls. But as it is the Light wherein we see, the Life that inspires us, the violence of His love, and the strength of our enjoyments, the greatness and perfection of every creature, the amplitude that enlargeth us, and the field wherein our thoughts expatiate without limit or restraint, the ground and foundation of all our satisfactions, the operative energy and power of the Deity; the measure of our delights, and the grandeur of our soul, it is more our treasure, and ought more abundantly to be delighted in. It surroundeth us continually on every side, it fills us, and inspires us. It is so mysterious, that it is wholly within us, and even then it wholly seems and is without us. It is more inevitably and constantly, more nearly and immediately our dwelling place, than our cities and kingdoms and houses. Our bodies themselves are not so much ours, or within us as that is. The immensity of God is an eternal tabernacle. Why then we should not be sensible of that as much as of our dwellings, I cannot tell, unless our corruption and sensuality destroy us. We ought always to feel, admire, and walk in it. It is more clearly objected to the eye of the soul, than our castles and palaces to the eye of the body. Those accidental buildings may be thrown down, or we may be taken from them, but this can never be removed, it abideth for ever. It is impossible not to be within it, nay, to be so surrounded as evermore to be in the centre and midst of it, wherever we can possibly remove, is inevitably fatal to every being. . . .

Eternity magnifies our joys exceedingly, for whereas things in themselves began, and quickly end; before they came, were never in being; do service but for few moments; and after they are gone pass away and leave us for ever, Eternity retains the moments of their beginning and ending within itself: and from everlasting to everlasting those things were in their times and places before God, and in all their circumstances eternally will be, serving Him in those moments wherein they existed, to those intents and purposes for which they were created. The swiftest thought is present with Him eternally: the creation and the day of judgment, His first consultation, choice and determination, the result and end of all just now in full perfection, ever beginning, ever passing, ever ending with all the intervals of space between things and things: As if those objects that arise many thousand years one after the other were all together. We also were ourselves before God eternally; and have the joy of seeing ourselves eternally beloved and eternally blessed, and infinitely enjoying all the parts of our blessedness; in all the durations of eternity appearing at once before ourselves, when perfectly consummate in the Kingdom of Light and Glory. The smallest thing by the influence of eternity, is made infinite and eternal. We pass through a standing continent or region of ages, that are already before us, glorious and perfect while we come to them. Like men in a ship we pass forward, the shores and marks seeming to go backward, though we move and they stand still. We are not with them in our progressive motion, but prevent the swiftness of our course, and are present with them in our understandings. Like the sun we dart our rays before us, and occupy those spaces with light and contemplation which we move towards, but possess not with our bodies. And seeing all things in the light of Divine knowledge, eternally serving God, rejoice unspeakably in that service, and enjoy it all.

THOMAS TRAHERNE (1637?–1674), the son of a shoemaker in Hereford, England, was educated at Oxford. He became rector at Credenhill, near Hereford, and subsequently chaplain to the Lord Keeper of the Seals of England. He was a student of the ancient writings of the church. His writings, principally poetry, express an unbounded love for all creation and a sense of wonder and delight. Most of Traherne's work remained unpublished for 250 years, until in 1896 a manuscript of his poetry and prose was discovered in a London bookshop.

Take Heart

BRUCE AND LORY LOCKERBIE—1990

CHRISTIANS DON'T NEED to live like losers in some vast comic dice game. Christians are never victims; in fact, Christians need never be either pessimistic or optimistic, as though somehow their ultimate destiny were still in doubt. For a Christian, the truly biblical virtue is *hopefulness* because our hope is secure in the promises of Jesus Christ, who has set us free from the fear of death.

When we board an airplane, we pray for God's protection in travel and for the wisdom of the pilot and crew. Then we buckle up, obeying federal law, and follow the flight attendants' instructions. If we were mere fatalists, we'd trust ourselves to luck and chance or fate, believing that such powers have already picked the date and that nothing can alter their indifferent will.

Christians believe otherwise. We have an obligation to the God who gave us life to conserve and preserve it responsibly. By our careful diet, by our habits of work and play, by our necessary sleep, by prudent medical maintenance, and by sensible choices, we live to God's glory for as long as that life can mirror its Maker.

But how can we ever be ready for death—our own or someone else's? Death is never convenient, never easy. Worst of all, death is never wholly painless. A toddler stumbles into an uncovered well; a casual passerby is struck by a ricocheting bullet from a drug dealer's weapon; a brilliant scholar is crushed by a falling tree; a promising young leader—an athlete, a gifted communicator with his peers, is cut down by heart disease; a young wife and mother, in seemingly perfect health, collapses and dies from a cerebral hemorrhage; a bus full of church youths is rammed by a drunk driver exploding and incinerating its occupants; a terrorist bomb brings down a plane—and the world mourns.

Why do we cry at funerals? Because, even as we may rejoice that the angels and saints are greeting our loved one, that Christ our brother is welcoming him or her home, we feel the pain of parting. We cry, just as Jesus Himself wept at the grave of His friend Lazarus. We cry for ourselves, perhaps for others who may be grieving even more deeply than we know because they have no faith in heavenly reunion. We cry because it is right to cry, that even in Satan's final writhings before he is finally put down, one more of God's creatures must be taken from us—no matter how temporarily. But we also cry in anticipation of that glorious day, when God himself shall wipe away all tears from their eyes; and there shall be no more death, neither sorrow, nor crying, neither shall be there any more pain: for the former things are passed away (see Revelation 21:4). Who wouldn't want to have a tear—one trembling tear—to fall when God Himself will wipe them all away?

Bruce Lockerbie, after thirty-five years of teaching and administering that ended in 1991, now leads a team of consultants called PAIDEIA [pie-day-ah], Inc., who offer comprehensive services to schools, colleges/universities/seminaries, as well as churches, helping agencies, and other nonprofit institutions. He received degrees in English and American Studies from New York University, and was awarded honorary degrees by Eastern University (1985) and Taylor University (1993). He is author, coauthor, or editor of forty books.

Lory Lockerbie was a teacher of health education in the Long Island public elementary schools for thirty years. The Lockerbies are the parents of three adult children—Don, Kevin, and Ellyn—and have three grandchildren. Bruce and Lory are active in the parish ministry of the Caroline church of Brookhaven, an evangelical Episcopal parish.

CHAPTER 9

The Heavenly City

The Golden Jerusalem of Heaven

BERNARD OF CLUNY— *circa 1125*

Jerusalem the golden, with milk and honey blest,
Beneath thy contemplation sink heart and voice oppressed.
I know not, O I know not, what joys await us there;
What radiancy of glory, what bliss beyond compare.

They stand, those halls of Zion, all jubliant with song,
And bright with many an angel, and all the martyr throng.
The prince is ever in them, the daylight is serene.
The pastures of the blessed are decked in glorious sheen.

O sweet and blessed country, the home of God's elect!
O sweet and blessed country that eager hearts expect!
Jesus in mercy bring us to that dear land of rest;
Who art, with God the Father and Spirit, ever blessed.

With jasper glow thy bulwarks, thy streets with emerald blaze;
The sardis and the topaz unite in thee their rays;
Thine ageless walls are bonded with amethyst unpriced;
The saints build up thy fabric, the cornerstone is Christ.

Jerusalem the glorious! Glory of the elect!
O dear and future vision that eager hearts expect!

Even now by faith I see thee, even here thy walls discern;
To thee my thoughts are kindled, and strive, and pant, and
yearn.

The morning shall awaken, the shadows flee away,
And each true-hearted servant shall shine as doth the day.
There God, our King and portion, in fullness of His grace,
We then shall see forever, and worship face to face.

Bernard of Cluny (early twelfth century), also known as Bernard of Morval, was a monk in the famous Abbey of Cluny, France, when it was at the height of its wealth and fame. He was known for his writings against the corruptions of his era. His *De Contemptu Mundi* was a long poem from which a number of hymns have been extracted, including "Jerusalem the Golden," which owes its use largely to John Mason Neale (1818–1866), ardent translator of older Latin and Greek hymnody.

Eternally in God's Presence

John Gilmore—1989

God originally created earth and declared it good. Through sin our planet has been spoiled. In the renovation of heaven and earth God will salvage what man spoiled. And it will be returned to the church for full use and enjoyment at a level that is hard to imagine (see 1 Corinthians 2:9). . . .

To be in God's presence eternally is not to be confined in a cell, but to be surrounded by One whose nature, gifts, and glory are the essence of liberty, variety, and symmetry.

We desire to dwell in heaven, not because of its cubic shape, its jasper walls, its golden streets, its pearly gates, or its dazzling light. Christians want to go to heaven to be with Jesus and to live forever with the Lord.

For biographical information on this author, see page 118.

A City of Praise

C. S. Lewis—1962

THE THING YOU LONG FOR summons you away from the self. Even the desire for the thing lives only if you abandon it. This is the ultimate law—the seed dies to live, the bread must be cast upon the waters, he that loses his soul will save it. But the life of the seed, the finding of the bread, the recovery of the soul, are as real as the preliminary sacrifice. Hence it is truly said of heaven "in heaven there is no ownership. If any there took upon him to call anything his own, he would straightway be thrust out into hell and become an evil spirit." But it is also said "To him that overcometh will I give . . . a white stone, and in the stone a new name written, which no man knoweth saving he that receiveth it" (Revelation 2:17). What can be more a man's own than this new name which even in eternity remains a secret between God and him? And what shall we take this secrecy to mean? Surely, that each of the redeemed shall forever know and praise some one aspect of the divine beauty better than any other creature can. Why else were individuals created, but that God, loving all infinitely, should love each differently? . . . If all experienced God in the same way and returned Him an identical worship, the song of the Church triumphant would have no symphony, it would be like an orchestra in which all the instruments played the same note. . . . Heaven is a city, and a Body, because the blessed remain eternally different: a society, because each has something to tell all the others—fresh and ever fresh news of the "My God" whom each finds in Him whom all praise as "Our God."

For biographical information on this author, see page 10.

Chapter 9

Let Me Dwell in Thee!

HORATIUS BONAR—LATE NINETEENTH CENTURY

Bathed in unfallen sunlight,
Itself a sun-born gem,
Fair gleams the glorious city,
The new Jerusalem!
City fairest,
Splendor rarest,
Let me gaze on thee!

Calm in her queenly glory,
She sits all joy and light;
Pure in her bridal beauty,
Her raiment festal-white!
Home of gladness,
Free from sadness,
Let me dwell in thee!

Shading her golden pavement
The tree of life is seen,
Its fruit-rich branches waving,
Celestial evergreen.
Tree of wonder,
Let me under
Thee forever rest!

Fresh from the throne of Godhead
Bright in its crystal gleam,
Bursts out the living fountain,
Swells on the living stream.
Blessed river,
Let me ever
Feast my eye on thee!

Streams of true life and gladness,
  Springs of all health and peace;
No harps by thee hang silent,
  nor happy voices cease.
    Tranquil river,
    Let me ever
      Sit and sing by thee!

River of God, I greet thee,
  Not now afar, but near;
My soul to thy still waters
  Hastes in its thirstings here.
    Holy river,
    Let me ever
      Drink of only thee!

HORATIUS BONAR (1808–1889) has been called "the prince of Scottish hymn-writers." He was a minister of the Free Church of Scotland, becoming moderator of the Free Church Assembly in 1883. An author of numerous books, he is remembered now as the writer of more than six hundred hymns, including "Here, O My Lord, I See Thee Face to Face" and "By the Cross of Jesus Standing."

Heaven

MARTIN DE HAAN—2007

I'M LOOKING FORWARD to long walks with good friends, shared meals without rushing, and endless laughter at no one's expense.

I'm anticipating meaningful work with plenty of time for reading, photography, fishing, and community service. For occasional entertainment I have written off stadiums and ballparks. If my hunch is right, competition between friends will be healthy in heaven. I'm wondering if there might even be hockey without fights, soccer without brawls, and basketball playoffs where losing well is valued as much as winning. There may even be a safe form of boxing and NASCAR.

Frivolous speculation? Maybe. Insulting to God? I hope not. I'm trying to imagine a heaven that builds on the good we know while leaving behind the evil.

As a child, I feared heaven would be boring. I missed the point of gold streets and pearly gates. As a 10-year-old, what I really liked doing most was playing baseball, collecting fossils, and hunting frogs.

In the years that followed, the deaths of family members and friends have changed the way I think about heaven. But I still have questions. What will we do after enjoying long embraces, tears of laughter, and catching up? My mind still locks up like an overloaded computer when I try to weigh imponderable questions about a hereafter that will last forever.

Ironically, what gives me the most peace of mind is not cutting loose my imagination, but rather learning to trust. I find rest in the thought that God doesn't want us to know what He has planned for us. I wouldn't be surprised to hear such a God say something like, "If I told you, I'd have to take you." Or, based on the apostle Paul's experience, "If I told you how good it's going to be, I'd have to make life more difficult for you now."

Paul seemed to imply as much when describing what he thought might have been an out-of-body experience. By his own admission, he wasn't sure what happened. But he said he was caught up to Paradise where he heard things he wasn't allowed to talk about (see 2 Corinthians 12:1–4). Apparently, whatever Paul heard was so exhilarating that it would have distracted him from an ongoing dependence upon the grace of God. So, for the duration of Paul's time on earth, the Lord of heaven let him suffer at the hand of Satan, to keep him on his knees (see 2 Corinthians 12:7–9).

I'm convinced that the God who taught Paul to depend on Him one day at a time is now teaching us to rely on Him for an eternity that is beyond our ability to understand.

So how much then does He want us to know?

Mart De Haan is the grandson of RBC founder Dr. M. R. De Haan, and the son of former president Richard W. De Haan. Having served at

RBC for more than thirty years, Mart is now heard regularly on the *Discover the Word* radio program and seen on *Day of Discovery* television. Mart is also a contributing writer for *Our Daily Bread* devotional, the Discovery Series Bible study booklets, and a monthly column on timely issues called "Been Thinking About."

O Jerusalem

HILDEGARD OF BINGEN—TWELFTH CENTURY

O Jerusalem, golden city,
robed in royal purple;
O edifice of highest excellence,
you are a light never darkened.
You are adorned in the dawn
and in the heat of the sun.
O blessed childhood
which gleams in the dawn,
and fair youth,
aflame in the sun.

Your windows, Jerusalem,
are carefully decorated
with topaz and sapphire.

Just as a mountain cannot be hidden;
but instead crowned with roses,
lilies and purple, in a true revelation.
O tender flower of the field,
O sweet juiciness of the apples,
O burden without weight,
let none bend a head to their breast in guilt.

In you sings the Holy Spirit,
with whom the angelic choir unites,

and through whom you are adorned
in the Son of God,
having no stain upon you.

O Jerusalem, your foundation is laid
with burning stones,
which are the tax-gatherers and sinners
who were lost sheep,
but discovered by the Son of God
they ran to you, and were placed in you.

Thus your walls blaze with living stones,
who with great efforts of good will
have flown like clouds into the sky.

And so your towers, O Jerusalem,
glitter and gleam with dawn,
and with sacred incandescence,
and with all the finery of God
which you do not lack, O Jerusalem.

Hildegard of Bingen (1098–1179), born into a noble family in what is now Germany, was educated in a monastery. After experiencing a vision of God at age forty-two, she established a convent. In addition to composing music for her own lyrics, she also wrote on spiritual subjects, nature, and healing and was widely respected as a visionary and adviser.

Prepared As a Bride

John F. MacArthur—1996

Eternal heaven will be different from the heaven where God now dwells. . . . God will renovate the heavens and the earth, merging His heaven with a new universe for a perfect dwelling-place that will be our home forever. In other words, heaven, the realm where God dwells, will expand to encompass the entire universe of creation, which will be fashioned into a perfect and glorious domain fit for the glory of heaven. The apostle Peter described this as the hope of every redeemed person: "We, according to his promise, look for new heavens and a new earth, wherein dwelleth righteousness" (2 Peter 3:13 KJV). . . .

John writes, "I John saw the holy city, new Jerusalem, coming down from God out of heaven, prepared as a bride adorned for her husband" (Revelation 21:2).

As John watches (Revelation 21), an entire city, magnificent in its glory, descends whole from heaven and becomes a part of the new earth. Heaven and earth are now one. The heavenly realm has moved its capital city intact to the new earth. Pay special attention to the key terms in this verse:

"Prepared" seems to imply that New Jerusalem had already been made ready before the creation of the new heavens and new earth. John does not say he saw the city being created. When he laid eyes on it, it was complete already. In other words, it was brought to the new earth from another place. Where is this place?

"Coming down from God out of heaven" indicates that the city—already complete and thoroughly furnished—descended to the new earth from the heavenly realm. . . . This occurs immediately after the new heaven and earth are created. New Jerusalem, the capital city of the eternal realm, descends right before John's eyes, out of the very realm of God, where it has already been "prepared." Who "prepared" it? Evidently this incredible heavenly city is precisely what our Lord spoke of when He told His disciples that He was going away to "prepare a place" for them (John 14:3). Now at the unveiling of the new heavens and new earth, the city is finally prepared and ready.

"As a bride adorned for her husband." This speaks of the glory of this unimaginable city. Just think, when our Lord fashioned the material universe at the beginning of time, He did it in seven days. He has been working on heaven for nearly two millennia. What a wonder it must be! The surpassing glory of this city is too rich to express in words.

For biographical information on this author, see page 25.

Chapter 9

The New Heavens and the New Earth

Randy Alcorn — 1999

Many assume heaven will be unlike earth. But why do we think this? God designed earth for human beings. And nearly every description of heaven includes references to earthly things—eating, music, animals, water, trees, fruits, and a city with gates and streets.

The Bible speaks of the new heavens and the new earth—not a *non*heavens and *non*earth. "New" doesn't mean fundamentally different, but vastly superior. If someone says, "I'm going to give you a new car," you'd get excited. Why? Not because you have no idea what a car is, but because you *do* know.

A new car doesn't mean a vehicle without a steering wheel, seats, doors, and tires. If it didn't have those, it wouldn't be a car. The new car is a better version of what you already have. Likewise, the new earth will be a far better version of this earth. That's why we can anticipate it. If we think of heaven as a place where disembodied spirits float around—which is never depicted in the Bible—we can't get excited about it. It's not a nonearth we long for—it's a *new* earth. And we long not for a nonbody but for a *new* body (see 2 Corinthians 5:1–4).

The promise of new heavens and a new earth is introduced in Isaiah. In the New Testament, John tells us more about it, and Peter speaks of the earth being burned, followed by "a new heaven and a new earth, the home of righteousness" (2 Peter 3:10–13). I understand this not as the absolute destruction of the planet, but the scorching of the surface and everything on it. It's as if an artist wiped paint away and started a new and better painting, but on the same canvas. As our resurrection bodies will be a superior recreation of our old ones, so the earth will be the old earth liberated from sin and decay (see Romans 8:19–22), radically and beautifully transformed.

Our beloved, Jesus, and our home, heaven. What a person! What a place! (What more could we possibly ask for?)

For biographical information on this author, see page 34.

Jerusalem, My Home!

JOHN HENRY HOPKINS JR.—MID-NINETEENTH CENTURY

Jerusalem, my Home,
I see thy walls arise;
Their jasper clear and sardine stone
Flash radiance through the skies.
In clouds of heaven-descending,
With angel train attending,
Thy gates of glistening pearl unfold
On streets of glassy gold.
No sun is there, no day or night;
But of seven-fold splendors bright,
Thy Temple is the LIGHT OF LIGHT,
Jerusalem, my Home.

Jerusalem, my Home,
Where shines the royal Throne,
Each king casts down his golden crown
Before the Lamb thereon.
Thence flows the crystal River,
And, flowing on forever
With leaves and fruits on either hand,
The Tree of Life shall stand.
In blood-washed robes, all white and fair
The Lamb shall lead His chosen there,
While clouds of incense fill the air,
Jerusalem, my Home.

Jerusalem, my Home,
Where saints in triumph sing,
While, tuned in tones of golden harps,
Heaven's boundless arches ring.
No more in tears and sighing
Our weak hosannas dying,

But hallelujahs loud and high
Roll thundering through the sky.
One chorus thrills their countless throngs
Ten thousand times ten thousand tongues
Fill them with overwhelming songs,
Jerusalem, my Home.

Jerusalem, my Home,
Thou sole all glorious Bride,
Creation shouts with joy to see
Thy Bridegroom at thy side:
The Man yet interceding,
His Hands and Feet yet bleeding,
And Him the billowy hosts adore
LORD GOD for evermore,
And "Holy, Holy, Holy," cry
The choirs that crowd thy courts on high,
Resounding everlastingly
Jerusalem, my Home.

Jerusalem, my home,
Where saints in glory reign,
Thy haven safe, O when shall I,
Poor storm-tossed pilgrim, gain?
At distance dark and dreary,
With sin and sorrow weary,
For thee I toil, for thee I pray,
For thee I long alway.
And lo! mine eyes shall see thee, too:
O rend in twain, thou veil of blue,
And let the Golden City through—
Jerusalem, my Home!

JOHN HENRY HOPKINS JR. (1820–1891), a native of Vermont, intended a career in law but instead graduated from General Theological

Seminary in New York and was ordained in the Episcopal Church. He taught music in his seminary, edited a church publication, and served as rector of two parishes in Pennsylvania. He wrote books on church music, but his most famous work is the carol "We Three Kings of Orient Are."

CHAPTER 10

Worship in Heaven

Earth and Heaven Unite in Praise

Attributed to Ignaz Franz—1768

Holy God, we praise thy Name;
Lord of all, we bow before Thee;
All on earth thy scepter claim,
All in heaven above adore thee.
Infinite thy vast domain,
Everlasting is thy reign.

Hark! the glad celestial hymn,
Angel choirs above are raising;
Cherubim and seraphim,
In unceasing chorus praising,
Fill the heavens with sweet accord:
Holy, holy, holy, Lord.

Lo! the apostolic train
Join thy sacred name to hallow;
Prophets swell the glad refrain,
And the white robed martyrs follow,
And from morn to set of sun,
Through the church the song goes on.

Holy Father, holy Son,
Holy Spirit: Three we name thee,
Though in essence only One;
Undivided God we claim Thee,
And adoring bend the knee
While we own the mystery.

Ignaz Franz (1719–1790), a Catholic priest of Silesia (formerly eastern Germany, now Poland), is remembered as a hymnologist and compiler. "Holy God, We Praise Thy Name," which joins the praise of heaven with that of the church on earth, has been widely used in Protestant as well as Catholic worship.

Heavenly Worship

Charles Haddon Spurgeon—1856

"I heard a voice from heaven, as the voice of many waters, and as the voice of a great thunder: and I heard the voice of harpers harping with their harps" (Revelation 14:2 KJV) singing—how loud and yet how sweet!

> *Have you never in time of storm beheld the sea, with its hundred hands, clapping them in gladsome adoration of the Most High?*

First, then, singing *how loud*! It is said to be "like the voice of many waters." Have you never heard the sea roar, and the fulness thereof? Have you never walked by the sea-side, when the waves were singing, and when every little pebble-stone did turn chorister, to make up music to the Lord God of hosts? And have you never in time of storm beheld the sea, with its hundred hands, clapping them in gladsome adoration of the Most High? Have you never heard the sea roar out his praise, when the winds were holding carnival—perhaps singing the dirge of mariners, wrecked far out on the stormy deep, but far more likely exalting God with their hoarse voice, and praising him who makes a thousand fleets sweep over them in safety, and writes his furrows on their own youthful brow? Have you never heard the rumbling and booming of ocean on the shore, when it has been lashed into fury and has been driven upon the cliffs? If you have, you have a faint idea of the melody of heaven. It was "as the voice of many waters." But do not suppose that it is the whole of the idea. It is not the voice of one ocean, but the voice of many, that is needed to give you an idea of the melodies of heaven. You are to suppose ocean piled upon ocean, sea upon sea,—the Pacific piled upon the Atlantic, the Arctic upon that, the Antarctic higher still, and so ocean upon ocean, all lashed to fury, and all sounding with a mighty voice the praise of God. Such is the singing of heaven. . . . But why so loud? The answer is, because there are so many there to sing. Nothing is more grand than the singing of multitudes. Many have been the persons who have told me that they could but weep when they heard you sing in this assembly, so mighty seemed the sound when all the people sang—

"Praise God from whom all blessings flow."

And, indeed, there is something very grand in the singing of multitudes. . . . Think, then, what must be the voice of those who stand on the boundless plains of heaven, and with all their might shout, "Glory and honour and power and dominion unto him that sitteth on the throne, and to the Lamb for ever and ever."

But note next, while it was a loud voice, how *sweet* it was. Noise is not music. There may be "a voice like many waters," and yet no music. It was sweet as well as loud; for John says, "I heard the voice of harpers harping with their harps." Perhaps the sweetest of all instruments is the harp. There are others which give forth sounds more grand and noble, but the harp is the sweetest of all instruments. I have sometimes sat to hear a skilful harper, till I could say, "I could sit and hear myself away," whilst with skilful fingers he touched the chords gently, and brought forth strains of melody which flowed like liquid silver, or like sounding honey into one's soul. Sweet, sweet beyond sweetness; words can scarcely tell how sweet the melody. Such is the music of heaven. No jarring notes there, no discord, but all one glorious harmonious song. . . .

Why is the song said to be a new song? . . . It will be a new song, because the saints were never in such a position before as they will be when they sing this new song. They are in heaven now; but the scene of our text is something more than heaven. It refers to the time when all the chosen race shall meet around the throne, when the last battle shall have been fought, and the last warrior shall have gained his crown. It is not now that they are thus singing, but it is in the glorious time to come, when all the hundred and forty and four thousand—or rather, the number typified by that number—will be all safely housed and all secure. I can conceive the period. Time was—eternity now reigns. The voice of God exclaims, "Are my beloved all safe?" The angel flies through paradise and returns with this message, "Yea, they are."

For biographical information on this author, see page 95.

Leisure for the Praises of God

AURELIUS AUGUSTINE—426

HOW GREAT SHALL BE THAT FELICITY, which shall be tainted with no evil, which shall lack no good, and which shall afford leisure for the praises of God, who shall be all in all! For I know not what other employment there can be where no lassitude shall slacken activity, nor any want stimulate to labor. I am admonished also by the sacred song, in which I read or hear the words, "Blessed are they that dwell in Thy house, O Lord; they will be still praising Thee." All the members and organs of the incorruptible body, which now we see to be suited to various necessary uses, shall contribute to the praises of God; for in that life necessity shall have no place, but full, certain, secure, everlasting felicity. For all those parts of the bodily harmony, which are distributed through the whole body, within and without, and of which I have just been saying that they at present elude our observation, shall then be discerned; and, along with the other great and marvellous discoveries which shall then kindle rational minds in praise of the great Artificer, there shall be the enjoyment of a beauty which appeals to the reason. What power of movement such bodies shall possess, I have not the audacity rashly to define, as I have not the ability to conceive. Nevertheless I will say that in any case, both in motion and at rest, they shall be, as in their appearance, seemly; for into that state nothing which is unseemly shall be admitted. One thing is certain, the body shall forthwith be wherever the spirit wills, and the spirit shall will nothing which is unbecoming either to the spirit or to the body. True honor shall be there, for it shall be denied to none who is worthy, nor yielded to any unworthy; neither shall any unworthy person so much as sue for it, for none but the worthy shall be there. True peace shall be there, where no one shall suffer opposition either from himself or any other. God Himself, who is the Author of virtue, shall there be its reward; for, as there is nothing greater or better, He has promised Himself. What else was meant by His word through the prophet, "I will be your God, and ye shall be my people," than, I shall be their satisfaction, I shall be all that men honorably desire,—life, and health, and nourishment, and plenty, and glory, and honor, and peace, and all good things? This, too, is the right interpretation of the saying of the apostle, "That God may be all in all." He shall be the end of our desires who shall be seen without end, loved without cloy, praised without weariness. This outgoing of affection, this employment, shall certainly be, like eternal life itself, common to all.

Aurelius Augustine (354–430) was born in North Africa to a Christian mother, Monica, and a pagan father. He fell away from his early nominal Christianity, but his career in rhetoric took him to Rome and then to Milan, where he came under the influence of the bishop Ambrose and was baptized in 387. Returning home to North Africa, Augustine was ordained a priest and became bishop of Hippo from 396 till his death. He worked on *De Civitate Dei (The City of God)* over a thirteen-year period, completing it in 426 when he was seventy-two. Through the centuries, Augustine's writings have influenced both Roman Catholic and Protestant theologians.

The End of All Sorrow

R. C. Sproul—1988

God will wipe away every tear from their eyes; there shall be no more death, nor sorrow, nor crying. There shall be no more pain, for the former things have passed away. (Revelation 21:4)

When I was a child my mother always ministered to me tenderly when I was hurt. When tears spilled out of my eyes I sobbed with uncontrollable spasms, my mother took her handkerchief and patted the tears from my cheeks. Often she would "kiss away the tears."

There are few more intimate human experiences than the physical act of wiping away another person's tears. It is a tactile act of compassion. It is a piercing form of nonverbal communication. It is the touch of consolation.

My mother dried my tears more than once. Her consolation worked for the moment and the sobbing subsided. But then I would get hurt again, and the tears would flow once more. My tear ducts still work. I still have the capacity to weep.

But when God wipes away tears, it is the end of all crying. John writes, "There shall be no more crying." Any tears shed in heaven could only be tears of joy. When God dries our eyes from all sorrowful weeping, the consolation will be permanent.

In heaven there will be no reason for mournful tears. Death will be no more. There will be no sorrow, no pain whatsoever. These things belong to the former things that shall pass away.

Then He who sat on the throne said, "Behold, I make all things new." And He said to me, "Write, for these words are true and faithful." (Revelation 21:5)

If anything sounds too good to be true, it is the announcement of the place where pain, sorrow, tears, and death are banished. The heart almost faints at the thought of it. We are almost afraid to think of it, lest we set ourselves up for a bitter disappointment. But the commanding voice from the imperial throne of God spoke decisively to John. "Write it down!" he ordered. "These words are true and faithful."

For biographical information on this author, see page 12.

The Redeemed Saints Worship

STEVEN J. LAWSON—1995

JOINING WITH THE ANGELS' ADORATION is the worship of all the redeemed saints in Heaven. The elders—representing all the saved of all the ages—now respond to the worship of the cherubim and join with them in praising God. Worship is always contagious—always! Perhaps it is the angels' greater proximity to the throne that leads John to record their worship first. As his eye scopes this scene, his sight moves away from the throne to these elders who immediately surround these angels.

If the angels reveal to us who we worship,
the elders show us how to worship.

If the angels reveal to us who we worship, the elders show us how to worship. We are not surprised to find these worshipers flat on their faces before God. People in the presence of God always fall down before Him. Seeing the unveiled glory of God always pulls the rug out from under prideful people and puts them belly down on their faces.

For biographical information on this author, see page 120.

Bless the Lord for His Saints!

William Walsham How—1864

For all Thy saints, who from their labours rest
Who Thee by faith before the world confessed,
Thy Name, O Jesu, be forever blessed.
Alleluia!

Thou wast their Rock, their Fortress, and their Might;
Thou, Lord, their Captain in the well-fought fight;
Thou, in the darkeness drear, their Light of light.
Alleluia!

For the Apostles' glorious company,
Who, bearing forth the cross o'er land and sea,
Shook all the mighty world,—we sing to Thee
Alleluia!

For the Evangelists, by whose blest word,
Like four-fold streams, the garden of the Lord
Is fair and fruitful,—be Thy Name adored.
Alleluia!

For Martyrs, who with rapture-kindled eye
Saw the bright crown descending from the sky,
And died to grasp it,—Thee we glorify.
Alleluia!

O may Thy soldiers, faithful still and bold,
Fight as the Saints who nobly fought of old,
And win, with them, the victors' crown of gold.
Alleluia!

O best communion! Fellowship divine!
We feebly struggle, they in glory shine;
Yet all are one in Thee, for all are Thine.
Alleluia!

And when the strife is fierce, the warfare long,
Steals on the ear the distant triumph-song,
And hearts are brave again, and arms are strong.
Alleluia!

The golden evening brightens in the west:
Soon, soon, to faithful warriors comes the rest;
Sweet is the calm of Paradise the blest.
Alleluia!

But lo! there breaks a yet more glorious Day:
The saints triumphant rise in bright array;
The King of Glory passes on His way.
Alleluia!

From earth's wide bounds, from ocean's farthest coast,
Through gates of pearl streams in the countless host,
Singing to Father, Son, and Holy Ghost.
Alleluia!

William Walsham How (1823–1897), an Anglican clergyman, served for twenty-eight years in Whittington. He published several books of poems and other writings, but is mostly remembered for his sixty hymn texts. Several remain in common use, including "O Jesus, Thou Art Standing," "O Word of God Incarnate," and "We Give Thee but Thine Own," but the best known is probably "For All the Saints" (originally, as here, "For All Thy Saints"). William W. How was consecrated bishop of Wakefield in 1888.

A Chosen Bride

ERWIN W. LUTZER—1998

THE ALMIGHTY WAS NOT CONTENT with the fellowship of the Trinity in eternity past. The Father, Son, and Holy Spirit were in eternal harmony in purpose and action; their relationship was beautiful and perfect. Yet apparently there was something missing—the fellowship of creatures would better display God's attributes. Mankind's plunge into sin would give God a gracious opportunity to showcase His love and intentions.

So the Almighty chose to clean up the mess Adam and Eve had created. Specifically, He had a Son named Christ, who would stand at the head of a whole new race of humanity. This Son is known as the "second Adam," for He will succeed where the first Adam failed. Adam was only a replica of God, but Christ is the perfect "image of the invisible God" (Colossians 1:15). Such a perfect image that He is, in fact, God.

Long before the Fall, God the Father promised a gift of redeemed humanity to His Son. The Son would purchase these people and they would be united as one body to share in His love and honor. And because this bride would be purchased at high cost by the Bridegroom, the intensity of the love would be evident for all to see.

Think this through. *Just as God sought a bride for Adam, so God sought a bride for His Son, Jesus Christ.* He chose to prepare a companion who would be able to share His Son's rule over the universe, someone who would enjoy His dominion. This bride would be loved, honored, and invited to join Christ on the throne of the universe. . . .

We are engaged to Christ, but someday we will be married to Him. We have in the Bible a rather detailed description of the "marriage supper of the Lamb" (Revelation 19:9 NASB), for which we must be properly dressed. . . .

" 'Let us rejoice and be glad and give the glory to Him, for the marriage of the Lamb has come and His bride has made herself ready.' And it was given to her to clothe herself in fine linen, bright and clean; for the fine linen is the righteous acts of the saints." (Revelation 19:7–8)

The righteous acts of the saints! What are these righteous acts? Certainly not the acts that declared us justified before God. . . . These are different garments.

In order to attend the marriage supper of the Lamb, we need two different suits of clothes. The first is the righteousness of Christ, the gift which admits us into heaven. This is a free set of clothes, the garments by which we are ushered into heaven's courts. "He made Him who knew no sin to be sin on our behalf, that we might become the righteousness of God in Him" (2 Corinthians 5:21 NASB).

But the second suit of clothes is a wedding garment for the marriage supper. . . . the deeds we have done for Christ on earth. Christ has made us ready for heaven; we must make ourselves ready for the wedding feast. We must distinguish between what only God can do and that which we can have a part in doing.

What are we doing today? We are sewing the garments that we shall wear at the marriage supper of the Lamb. We are making sure that we will not be so scantily clad that we shall be ashamed.

For biographical information on this author, see page 136.

The Feast of Salvation

MAGNUS B. LANDSTAD—1861

Full many shall come from the east and the west
And sit at the feat of salvation,
With Abraham, Isaac, and Jacob the blest,
Obeying the Lord's invitation.
Have mercy upon us, O Jesus!

But they who have always resisted His grace
And on their own virtue depended
Shall then be condemned and cast out from His face,
Eternally lost and unfriended.
Have mercy upon us, O Jesus!

May we too give heed when our Saviour doth call
In accents persuasive and tender,
And may we be guests at His feast, one and all,
Our praise and obeisance to render.
Have mercy upon us, O Jesus!

Oh, that we the throng of the ransomed may swell,
To who He hath granted remission!
God graciously make us in heaven to dwell
And save us from endless perdition.
Have mercy upon us, O Jesus!

God grant that I may of His infinite love
Remain in His merciful keeping
And sit with the King at His table above
When here in the grave I am sleeping.
Have mercy upon us, O Jesus!

Then ended will be, like a dream that is past,
All trial and trouble and sorrow;
All questions and doubts will be answered at last,
When dawneth eternity's morrow.
Have mercy upon us, O Jesus!

Then heaven will ring with an anthem more grand
Then ever on earth was recorded,
When all of the saved shall receive at his hand
The crown to the victors awarded.
Have mercy upon us, O Jesus!

Magnus Brostrup Landstad (1802–1880) was a Norwegian Lutheran pastor. Ordained in 1827, he served several parishes and spent his last years in Oslo (then called Kristiana). He worked on a hymnal for the Lutheran Church of Norway, which was published in 1869. Earlier, he issued a collection of folk songs (1852–1853).

Chapter 10

Unbroken Fellowship with God

JONI EARECKSON TADA—1995

WITHOUT QUESTION, the most marvelous thing of all about heaven—heaven's supreme delight—will be unbroken fellowship with God Himself.

First John 1:3 defines our salvation in terms of fellowship with God: "Our fellowship is with the Father, and with his Son Jesus Christ." When we become believers, we enter into close spiritual fellowship with God. His life becomes ours. His will becomes our will, and His purpose our purpose. Even though sin hinders our walk with Christ on earth, the deepest part of our regenerated soul is united with the living God and in fellowship with the living Christ.

In other words, salvation brings us into communion with God. We can talk and commune with Him. We pray to Him as our dear Father—"Abba," in Paul's favorite terminology. We hear Him speak to us in His Word. He moves providentially in our lives to reveal Himself. We enjoy real spiritual communion with Him.

But that communion is nonetheless incomplete, shrouded from our plain view. As Paul writes, "Now we see through a glass, darkly; but then face to face: now I know in part; but then shall I know even as also I am known" (1 Corinthians 13:12 KJV). He's talking about our fellowship with God. In heaven it will be perfect, unhindered, unclouded by any sin or darkness. . . .

The closer we draw to the Lord Jesus and the more we set our hearts and minds on heavenly glories above, the better prepared we shall be for heaven's perfection. Fellowship won't mean sitting at the feet of Jesus and fighting back boredom while everyone else is enraptured. No. Fellowship will be the best of what earthly friendship merely hinted at. . . .

Heaven's Wedding Supper of the Lamb will be the perfect party. The Father has been sending out invitations and people have been RSVP-ing through the ages. Jesus has gone ahead to hang the streamers, prepare the feast, and make our mansion ready. And like any party, what will make it sweet is the fellowship.

Fellowship with our glorious Savior and with our friends and family.

For biographical information on this author, see page 22.

Union of the Soul with God

FRANCIS DE SALES—1616

ALL THE RIVERS FLOW INCESSANTLY, and, as the wise man says: *Unto the place from whence they come they return to flow again.* The sea which is the place whence they spring, is also the place of their final repose; all their motion tends no farther than to unite themselves to their fountain. "O God," says S. Augustine, "thou hast created my heart for thyself, and it can never repose but in thee." *For what have I in heaven, and besides thee what do I desire upon earth? Thou art the God of my heart, and the God that is my portion for ever.* Still the union which our heart aspires to cannot attain to its perfection in this mortal life; we can commence our loves in this, but we can consummate them only in the other.

In this mortal life the soul is truly espoused and betrothed to the immaculate Lamb, but not as yet married to him.

The heavenly Spouse makes a delicate expression of this. *I found him whom my soul loveth,* says she, *I held him and I will not let him go, till I bring him into my mother's house, and into the chamber of her that bore me.* She finds him then, this well-beloved, for he makes her feel his presence by a thousand consolations; she holds him, for these feelings cause in her strong affections, by which she clasps and embraces him, protesting that she will never let him go,—O no! for these affections turn into eternal resolutions; yet she cannot consider that she kisses him with the nuptial kiss till she meet with him in her mother's house, which is the heavenly Jerusalem, as S. Paul says. But see, Theotimus, how this spouse thinks of nothing less than of keeping her beloved at her mercy as a slave of love; whence she imagines to herself that it is hers to lead him at her will, and to introduce him into her mother's happy abode; though in reality it is she who must be conducted thither by him, as was Rebecca into Sara's chamber by her dear Isaac. The spirit urged by amorous passion always gives itself a little advantage over what it loves; and the spouse himself confesses: *Thou hast wounded my heart, my sister, my spouse, thou hast wounded my heart with one of thy eyes, and with one hair of thy neck:* acknowledging himself her prisoner by love.

This perfect conjunction then of the soul with God, shall only be in heaven, where as the Apocalypse says, the Lamb's marriage feast shall be made. In this mortal life the soul is truly espoused and betrothed to the immaculate Lamb, but not as yet married to him: the troth is plighted, and promise given, but the execution of the marriage is deferred: so that we have always time, though never reason, to withdraw from it; our faithful spouse never abandons us unless we oblige him to it by our disloyalty and unfaithfulness. But in heaven the marriage of this divine union being celebrated, the bond which ties our hearts to their sovereign principle shall be eternally indissoluble.

FRANCIS BONAVENTURE (1567–1622), known as FRANCIS DE SALES, was the eldest son of the Count de Sales, in Savoy (southeastern France). He earned a doctorate in law, but then entered the priesthood in 1593. In 1602 he was made bishop of Genoa. His devotional writings arose from his pastoral concern for helping people live their ordinary lives in holiness.

The Roar of Praise

CALVIN MILLER—1996

IN PARADISE LOST the fallen prince, Lucifer, is asked what he most missed about the paradise he had lost. He is quick to reply, "the sound of trumpets in the morning." Milton must be right. Trumpets are the instruments of heaven. Their loud, strong voices cry out the presence of the city's unforsaking King. Violins may introduce a nocturne and harps may call forth spring, but only trumpets have the clear and certain voice to sound the approach of kings.

Who can remember the form of life we shared with others before our memories began. I had a brother, five years older than myself. We must have played for hours, but all of that is lost to me. My brother went one day with childhood friends to swim in a farm pond not far from where we lived. He never came home again. After the shock and numbness, a million questions came to us. Did his struggle to breathe overcome his reason with final terror? When his drowning struggle ended, did he meet the Christ who blessed the children?

I think I heard the bells of trumpets blare the thunder of heaven's reassurance. The first time I heard it was when I was but a child—a child so small that memory all but starts there. Have you visited that first place where the mind remembers anything? I have.

My ten-year-old brother was gone. I was barely five years old when my mother lifted me above his casket for a final look.

"Not coming back," she said.

"Where is he that he can't come back?" I asked.

"Heaven."

"Is it far from Garfield County?"

"Not far." She smiled.

I heard them sing at the funeral. I can't remember what they sang, but it must have been the old hymn "Beulah Land." I remember my mother singing that hymn so often over the next few years.

> Oh Beulah Land, sweet Beulah Land,
> As on a mighty rock I stand,
> I look away across the sea
> Where mansions are prepared for me
> And glimpse the heavenly glory shore,
> My hope, my heav'n forevermore.

She sang it all the time. I don't know why she sang. Perhaps grief can't quit hurting until it starts singing. She'd often stop and listen when she'd finish singing. Maybe she heard the thunder of some distant place. Maybe not, but she seemed so oddly silent as she sang. She seemed to stop to listen, and then she'd listen and sing. But in her odd litany of song and silence, she made me wonder if we are not most like heaven when we're singing. I've wondered if my little brother, who wasn't too far away, wasn't hearing some kind of continual music. I suppose if praise is the unending thunder of heaven, it's because heaven is filled with people who did a lot of grieving before they got there. It was grief that taught them the music even as heaven perfected their words. And the thunder rolls and trumpets speak clear notes of glory when the praise becomes so majestic that worlds can't say it anymore.

That's why the beasts of the Apocalypse fall down and cry: "Holy, holy, holy is the Lord God Almighty, who was, and is, and is to come" (Revelation 4:8).

Nor can the elders stand. They too sing best with their faces to the ground.

> You are worthy, our Lord and God,
> to receive glory and honor and power,
> for you created all things,
> and by your will they were created
> and have their being. (Revelation 4:11)

And the roar of praise thickens as all the angels in heaven join in the singing:

> Worthy is the Lamb, who was slain,
> to receive power and wealth and wisdom and
> strength
> and honor and glory and praise! (Revelation 5:12)

The elders seated on their thrones before God; fell on their faces and sang:

> We give thanks to you, Lord God Almighty
> the One who is and who was,

because you have taken your great power
and have begun to reign. (Revelation 11:17)

That's why Isaiah's seraphim fly and cry, as clear as gold trumpets: "Holy, holy, holy . . . the whole earth is full of his glory" (Isaiah 6:3).

Who would not enter this city singing? Who would not welcome the chance to exalt this King of Glory? Who has not at quiet midnights heard the glorious distant thunder of unending praise? I heard it as a boy of five. I'm not sure I would have heard it if my mother had not assured me heaven wasn't far from Garfield County.

I've never found it hard to believe in heaven. I've felt the quadraphonic rumble of God's tremolo. I've heard the distant thunder of praise. When the thunder died and I was no longer sure I had really heard it, I could still hear my mother. . . .

When she finally died I knew she held again that little boy, whose small earthly remains, like her own, lie yet in Garfield County. They must have smiled and studied each other in a lingering embrace of joy. Then they must have joined the unending praise breaking in the air around them. And then who can say? Perhaps the child, with his decades of practice, might have taught his mother the better music.

For biographical information on this author, see page 53.

Wondrous Love

American Folk Hymn
(attributed to Alexander Means)—1853

What wondrous love is this, O my soul, O my soul!
What wondrous love is this, O my soul!
What wondrous love is this that caused the Lord of bliss
To bear the dreadful curse for my soul, for my soul,
To bear the dreadful curse for my soul.

To God and to the Lamb I will sing, I will sing;
To God and to the Lamb I will sing.
To God and to the Lamb Who is the great "I AM,"
While millions join the theme, I will sing, I will sing,
While millions join the theme, I will sing.

And when from death I'm free, I'll sing on, I'll sing on;
And when from death I'm free, I'll sing on.
And when from death I'm free, I'll sing and joyful be,
And thru eternity, I'll sing on, I'll sing on,
And thro' eternity, I'll sing on.

An Audience of One

RANDY ALCORN — 1998

WE REJOINED OUR COMRADES in the great camp of Charis, embracing and shedding tears and slapping each other on the back. Then warriors around me turned toward the masses of untold millions gathered in Charis. The army began to sing, perhaps hundreds of thousands, perhaps a million.

"Elyon miriel o aeron galad, chara domina beth charis o aleathes celebron!"

I added my voice to theirs and sang the unchained praises of the King. Only for a moment did I hear my own voice, amazed to detect the increased intensity of the whole. One voice, even mine, made a measurable difference. But from then on I was lost in the choir, hardly hearing my voice and not needing to.

As we sang to the gathered throngs of Charis, the sheer power of their voices, *our* voices, nearly bowled me over.

Then suddenly the multitudes before us sang back to us, and our voices were drowned by theirs. We who a moment earlier seemed the largest choir ever assembled now proved to be only the small worship ensemble that led the full choir of untold millions, now lost to themselves. We sang together in full voice, "To him who made the galaxies, who became the Lamb, who stretched out on the tree, who crossed the chasm, who returned the Lion! Forever!"

The song's harmonies reached out and grabbed my body and my soul. I became the music's willing captive.

I knew now that all my life I had caught occasional strains of the music of Charis. But it was elusive, more like an echo. All that clatter, all those competing sounds, all the CDs and sitcoms and ringing phones and blowing horns and nagging voices drowned out the real music. I'd spent my life humming the wrong tunes, dancing to the wrong beat, marching to the wrong anthem.

No longer—for at long last I heard, undiluted, the song for which I was made. And I not only heard the song, I sang it!

The galaxies and nebulae sang with us the royal song. It echoed off a trillion planets and reverberated in a quadrillion places in every nook and cranny of the universe. The song generated the light of a billion burning supernovae. It blotted out all lesser lights and brought a startling clarity to the way things really were. It didn't blind, it illuminated, and I saw as never before.

At long last, things *were* as they appeared.

Our voices broke into thirty-two distinct parts, and instinctively I knew which of them I was made to sing. "We sing for joy at the work of your hands . . . we stand in awe of you." It felt indescribably wonderful to be lost in something so much greater than myself.

There was no audience, I thought for a moment, for audience and orchestra and choir all blended into one great symphony, one grand cantata of rhapsodic melodies and powerful sustaining harmonies.

No, wait, there *was* an audience. An audience so vast and all-encompassing that for a moment I'd been no more aware of it than a fish is aware of water.

I looked at the great throne, and upon it sat the King . . . the Audience of One.

The smile of his approval swept through the choir like fire across dry wheat fields.

When we completed our song, the one on the throne stood and raised his great arms and clapped his scarred hands together in thunderous applause, shaking ground and sky, jarring every corner of the cosmos. His applause went on and on, unstopping and unstoppable.

And in that moment I knew, with unwavering clarity, that the King's approval was all that mattered—and ever would.

For biographical information on this author, see page 34.

Unending Praise

ISAAC WATTS—1719

I'll praise my Maker with my breath;
And when my voice is lost in death,
  Praise shall employ my nobler powers;
My days of praise shall ne'er be past,
While life, and thought, and being last,
  Or immortality endures

Why should I make a man my trust?
Princes must die and turn to dust:
  Vain is the help of flesh and blood;
Their breath departs, their pomp and power,
And thoughts all vanish in an hour;
  Nor can they make their promise good.

Happy the man whose hopes rely
On Israel's God: He made the sky,
  And earth and seas with all their train;
His truth forever stands secure:
He saves the oppress'd, he feeds the poor;
  And none shall find his promise vain.

The Lord hath eyes to give the blind;
The Lord supports the sinking mind;
  He sends the labouring conscience peace;
He helps the stranger in distress,

The widow and the fatherless,
    And grants the prisoner sweet release.

He loves his saints, he knows them well,
But turns the wicked down to hell:
    Thy God, O Zion, ever reigns;
Let every tongue, let every age,
In this exalted work engage;
    Praise him in everlasting strains.

I'll praise him while he lends me breath,
And when my voice is lost in death,
    Praise shall employ my nobler powers.
My days of praise shall ne'er be past,
While life, and thought, and being last,
    Or immortality endures.

Isaac Watts (1674–1748) was born in Southampton, England, into a family who were Dissenters from the Church of England. Isaac began learning Latin at four years of age and went on to learn Greek and Hebrew as well, but could not enjoy a university education because of his dissent from the established church. Most of the free churches sang only metrical psalms in their worship, but singing in England had declined in quality. Watts made a fresh start with psalm paraphrases that rhymed, and were "evangelical," introducing the gospel of Christ into psalm-singing. He wrote more than six hundred such hymns. Among his best known today are "Jesus Shall Reign," "Our God, Our Help in Ages Past," and "When I Survey the Wondrous Cross."

CHAPTER 11

Not in Heaven

Faith in the Future

JOE BEAM—2000

The Holy Spirit penned words through Paul to give us faith in the future, beyond this life. Therefore we do not lose heart. Though outwardly we are wasting away, yet inwardly we are being renewed day by day. For our light and momentary troubles are achieving for us an eternal glory that far outweighs them all. So we fix our eyes not on what is seen, but on what is unseen. For what is seen is temporary, but what is unseen is eternal.

Now we know that if the earthly tent we live in is destroyed, we have a building from God, an eternal house in heaven, not built by human hands. Meanwhile we groan, longing to be clothed with our heavenly dwelling, because when we are clothed, we will not be found naked. For while we are in this tent, we groan and are burdened, because we do not wish to be unclothed but to be clothed with our heavenly dwelling, so that what is mortal may be swallowed up by life. (2 *Corinthians* 4:16–5:4)

BY FAITH WE BELIEVE what God said through Paul. The bodies we live in are meant for this realm—temporary tents meant for this world. These tents will fold. Our resurrection bodies will be vastly different. Paul told the Corinthians in his previous letter, "So will it be with the resurrection of the dead. The body that is sown is perishable, it is raised imperishable; it is sown in dishonor, it is raised in glory; it is sown in weakness, it is raised in power; it is sown a natural body, it is raised a spiritual body. If there is a natural body, there is also a spiritual body" (1 Corinthians 15:42–44).

Imperishable, glorious, powerful, spiritual: That's the resurrection body for all who choose to live with God in eternity.

That's the body Angel will have.

You see, there is no such thing as retardation in heaven—such handicaps exist in this realm only. Angel's brain doesn't work right because her body is perishable, weak, and natural. It is subject to decay (see Romans 8:20–21). Her spirit is just as full and healthy as any other; it is simply trapped in a malfunctioning body.

When she dies—and as selfish parents we hope that doesn't happen for many, many years—she will be freed from the retardation that now affects her body. There isn't a special education section in heaven. There, at *last,* she can express all the things her mind can't get right now. She tries to tell us what she feels, how she thinks, but her brain works against her. She communicates on a simple, childish level. Someday, when Alice and I sit in heaven with her, we'll have all those conversations we wanted to have here—heart to heart, mind to mind.

Think about it and rejoice.

A baby isn't a baby after he dies; he's full-grown in heaven because being a baby is a function of the flesh. There aren't any nurseries in heaven—no children's church; no monumental mountain of non-decaying plastic diapers; no angels preparing formula in the kitchen, squeezing drops onto their wrists to make sure the temperature is just right.

Children who die of starvation aren't fattened up at a giant banquet table in heaven. Whole, healthy people enter the gates of Paradise.

Older people suffering from memory loss because of Alzheimer's regain all those precious memories the moment they die. Paraplegics can run, jump, and dance before God. The deaf will cry joyously as they hear the harmony of the angelic chorus. The mute will join in, testing their new voices, still signing their words out of habit until they realize they need never sign again.

I can see all those things as I close my eyes and dream in faith. I believe.

For biographical information on this author, see page 50.

No Curse

HERBERT LOCKYER—1980

IT IS GENERALLY KNOWN that the Bible begins and ends with gardens. What is not realized as it should be, is that the curse associated with the initial garden is missing from the last garden. . . . In the Garden of Eden there was one tree that God forbade Adam and Eve to pluck fruit from or even touch; but Eve knew its fruit was nutritious, as well as beneficial to the mind. Such a participation brought a curse upon Satan, as well as a curse upon the human race and the expulsion of our first parents from the garden. . . .

The glory of the Gospel, however, is the blessed fact that Christ took our curse and made it His own. . . . Curse and death came through a tree, but, at Calvary, blessing and life came through Him who hung on a tree. . . . How thrilled John was when—with earth's first garden and its curse in mind—the Lord gave him a glimpse of the heavenly garden, in which there was no more curse.

HERBERT LOCKYER (1886–1984) spent nearly three decades as a pastor in England and Scotland before coming to the United States. He conducted a ten-year lecturing ministry under the auspices of Moody Bible Institute, and was the author of more than fifty books.

It Will Be Worth It All

William J. Gaither—1966

There's a promised land made for all the free,
When our race on earth is run,
Where no broken dreams will mar our memory;
It will be worth it all when we get home.

There no sad farewells, there no tear-stained eyes,
There no heart-ache, grief, or woe,
There no shattered hopes will ever cloud the skies;
It will be worth it all when we get home.

It will be worth it all just to see His face,
When He claims us for His own;
Then ten million years to sing amazing grace;
It will be worth it all when we get home.

William J. Gaither's illustrious career in music began when he formed his first group, The Bill Gaither Trio, while he was still a college student. In subsequent years, he has written more than five hundred songs, released more than forty albums, and has produced more than fifty videos.

No Needs

John F. MacArthur—1996

In Revelation 22:1–2 the angel shows John "a pure river of water of life, clear as crystal, proceeding out of the throne of God and of the Lamb. In the midst of the street of it, and on either side of the river, was there the tree of life, which bare twelve manner of fruits, and yielded her fruit every month: and the leaves of the tree were for the healing of the nations" (KJV). This crystal-clear, celestial river flows out of the throne and through the middle of the New Jerusalem. Imagine what a river meant to someone living in a barren place like Palestine. It was a welcome place of comfort and rest, refreshment and sustenance. A river meant cool water to a mouth parched by the desert heat. Cities were built next to rivers. And imagine the joy of someone who lived in the desert finding a tree with fruit! The New Jerusalem will be the epitome of everything precious—a city, a river, and trees. . . .

In heaven we will eat for enjoyment, not sustenance. Nevertheless, the [fruit of the] tree has a wholesome, beneficial effect on those who partake. . . . The water of life is also there for the sheer pleasure of drinking. No food will be *needed* in heaven, but incredible gourmet delights will nonetheless be enjoyed. Again this underscores that truth the God's design for us is that we may *enjoy* Him forever. Much of heaven is designed for sheer pleasure—both the pleasure of God and the pleasure of His people.

For biographical information on this author, see page 25.

No Regret in Heaven

L. L. Hamline—mid-nineteenth century

In that blessed world the sins of this life will inflict upon the soul neither remorse nor repentance. Here gracious hearts are filled with godly sorrow at the remembrance of transgression and the remains of carnal appetite. But the hearts of the glorified will not lament. The just made perfect will feel no repentance, and the sanctified and spotless will have no carnal tempers. Now sin provokes in the believers self-reproach and indignation. Such cannot forgive themselves, even when God forgives them. They abhor themselves like Job, and repent as in sack-cloth. Their penitence is not distrustful and death-working, like the sinner's, but still it is penitence; and they are unwilling to part from it all the days of their life. The happiest hours of the best Christians are softened by this penitence. They may have ascended the mount of regeneration, the mount of faith, the mount of love; but on the loftiest summit they shall find no soil barren of repentance, no region so clear and lofty as never to see a cloud, or feel the refreshing moisture of its gently-falling showers. Our earthly graces are moral buds and blossoms. They are most beautiful and fragrant when watered with drops of generous sorrow. When these buds of grace become the ripened fruits of glory, they can endure perpetual sunshine. There they will be garnered in a tearless heaven.

Our earthly graces are moral buds and blossoms. . . .
When these buds of grace become the ripened fruits of glory,
they can endure perpetual sunshine.

Leonidas Lent Hamline (1797–1865), born in Connecticut, began his ministry as a Methodist circuit rider in southern Ohio and served as an editor of Methodist publications. In 1842 he had an experience of sanctification, and the promotion of holiness became his emphasis for the remainder of his ministry. Hamline was elected a bishop in 1844. He was concerned with the approach of the millennium, which in his thinking was linked with the sanctification of God's people. Hamline University, St. Paul, Minnesota, bears his name.

Only Radiance in the New Life

Harriet Beecher Stowe—1859

As there was an hour when the fishermen of Galilee saw their Master transfigured, His raiment white and glistening, and His face like the light, so are there hours when our whole mortal life stands forth in the celestial radiance. From our daily lot falls off every weed of care—from our heart-friends every speck and stain of earthly infirmity. Our horizon widens, and blue and amethyst and gold touch every object. Absent friends and friends gone on the last long journey stand once more together, bright with an immortal glow, and like the disciples who saw their Master floating in the clouds above them, we say, "Lord, it is good to be here!" How fair the wife, the husband, the absent mother, the grey-haired father, the manly son, the bright-eyed daughter! Seen in the actual present, all have some fault, some flaw; but absent, we see them in their permanent and better selves. Of our distant home we remember not one dark day, not one servile care, nothing but the echo of its holy hymns and the radiance of its brightest days—of our father, not one hasty word, but only the fulness of his manly vigour and noble tenderness—and of our mother, nothing of mortal weakness, but a glorified form of love—of our brother, not one teasing, provoking word of brotherly freedom, but the proud beauty of his noblest hours—of our sister, our child, only what is fairest and sweetest.

This is to life the true ideal, the calm glass wherein looking, we shall see that, whatever defects cling to us, they are not, after all, permanent, and that we are tending to something nobler than we yet are:—it is "the earnest of our inheritance until the redemption of the purchased possession." In the resurrection we shall see our friends for ever as we see them in these clairvoyant hours.

Harriet Beecher Stowe (1811–1896) was the daughter of preacher Lyman Beecher, founder of the American Bible Society. After the family moved from Connecticut to Cincinnati, she married Calvin Stowe. Harriet worked as a writer for local and religious periodicals. Her literary output included poems, travel books, children's books, and ten novels, the most famous being *Uncle Tom's Cabin,* which she completed after moving with her husband to Brunswick, Maine. The Stowes lost four of their seven children.

Release from Pain

Julian of Norwich—1393

Before this time I had often great longing, and desired of God's gift to be delivered from this world and this life, for I wanted to be with my God in the bliss in which I surely hope to be without end. For often I beheld the woe that there is here, and the good and the blessed life that is there; and if there had been no other pain on earth except the absence of our Lord God, it seemed to me sometimes that that would be more than I could bear. And this made me mourn and diligently long.

Then God said to me, for my patience and endurance: Suddenly you will be taken out of all your pain, all your unrest and all your woe. And you will come up above, and you will have me for your reward, and you will be filled full of joy and bliss, and you will never have any kind of pain, any kind of sickness, any kind of displeasure, any kind of disappointment, but always endless joy and bliss. Why then should it grieve you to endure for awhile, since it is my will and to my glory?

JULIAN OF NORWICH (1342–ca.1416), also called MOTHER or DAME JULIAN, was an English mystic and hermitess. Her *Showings,* on which she worked for twenty years, is based on a revelation of Christ she experienced in 1373, when she was thirty years old. *Showings,* also known as *Revelations of Divine Love,* is a classic of English mysticism. Its dominant ideas are the great love of God and the detestable nature of human sin.

No More Good-byes

DAVID HANEY—1999

REBECCA WAS ONE of the most beautiful young women I have ever known. She had the kind of beauty that transcended her attractive appearance. Her beauty radiated from her heart. She was intelligent, intensely spiritual, extremely talented, and unwavering in her pursuit of excellence. . . . She was the pride and joy of her parents and a prized friend of all who knew her.

Her beauty was taken from us this past Wednesday. In one of those tragic events that plague our mutinous planet, her life ended in an unrepeatable instant. Without warning, without explanation, without anticipation, as she walked along a familiar road, she inadvertently stepped out in front of an oncoming automobile, and before she could have realized her mistake, she was gone. . . .

As family and friends gathered in that all-too-familiar context of sorrow, Rebecca's father and I went into a side room to talk and make arrangements for the days ahead. We spoke to people from all over the country—some who knew this beautiful young woman and some who simply knew of her. Her father's resolve in the face of this tragedy was overwhelming. The depth of his pain and the significance of his loss were as great as any we can know.

After one of the phone calls, he quietly hung up, turned to me, and said, "I guess that's the point, Dave."

"Excuse me?" I imagined I had missed the first part of his statement.

"The point of this kind of thing. The point of heaven," he said.

My puzzled look urged him to continue. "Heaven. That's the point—heaven. More than ever, that is where I want to be—where I can see her again and talk to her again and . . . hold her again."

He paused as if momentarily transported to that place and that day. Then he finished, "Now the rest of my life will just be waiting."

As his lip trembled and his eyes pressed closed, I got the point.

For biographical information on this author, see page 47.

Beyond Dying

Sara Teasdale—1920

If I must go to heaven's end
    Climbing the ages like a stair,
Be near me and forever bend
    With the same eyes above me there;
Time will fly past us like leaves flying,
    We shall not heed, for we shall be
Beyond living, beyond dying,
    Knowing and known unchangeably.

Sarah Teasdale (1884–1933) was born in St. Louis. Thought to be frail by her family, she was sheltered as a child from much of the outside world. She was self-analytical, and as her poetry developed, it transitioned from the genteel style of nineteenth-century female poets into highly personal lyrics, sometimes shocking for her time, that explored adult emotions. Like Christina Rossetti and Emily Dickinson, Sara Teasdale tended to create her poetry in seclusion. A lack of self-esteem plagued her throughout life, despite growing recognition. In 1918 her *Love Songs* won what was essentially the first Pulitzer Prize for Poetry.

CHAPTER 12

Influence of Heaven

Living under Heaven

M. Craig Barnes—1997

According to a recent Gallup poll, the majority of Americans believe in a literal heaven. Most of the people surveyed said that they expect it to be a continuation of life on earth but without the wars, disease, death, and other inconveniences that cramp their present pursuit of happiness.

Heaven is not just a place we go to when we die. Heaven . . . gives meaning and order to the earth that sits beneath it.

If heaven is something that is simply waiting at the end of time, or at least at the end of our time, then it is easy to say we believe in it. But that isn't the real question that Scripture asks you. The real question is, do you live under heaven?

The biblical perspective on heaven and earth is not linear as if earth comes first, and then heaven. Rather it is vertical, so that all humanity exists on the earth and under heaven. The reason that is important is that heaven is not just a place we go to when we die. Heaven is also a place that gives meaning and order to the earth that sits beneath it. . . .

In a world that is divorced from heaven, the only reality is what we see. The only relationships we have are with those who are still alive. It isn't enough. Those who live under heaven, by contrast, enjoy a world where grace is a frequent invader.

M. Craig Barnes is pastor of Shadyside Church in Pittsburgh, Pennsylvania. He teaches at Pittsburgh Theological Seminary and has authored several books.

Seeking the Heavenly Life

Clement—*circa* 97

How blessed and wonderful, beloved, are the gifts of God! Life in immortality, splendor in righteousness, truth in perfect confidence, faith in assurance, self-control in holiness! And all these fall under the cognizance of our understandings [now]; what then shall those things be which are prepared for such as wait for Him? The Creator and Father of all worlds, the Most Holy, alone knows their amount and their beauty. Let us therefore earnestly strive to be found in the number of those that wait for Him, in order that we may share in His promised gifts. But how, beloved, shall this be done? If our understanding be fixed by faith towards God; if we earnestly seek the things which are pleasing and acceptable to Him; if we do the things which are in harmony with His blameless will; and if we follow the way of truth, casting away from us all unrighteousness and iniquity, along with all covetousness, strife, evil practices, deceit, whispering, and evil-speaking, all hatred of God, pride and haughtiness, vainglory and ambition. For they that do such things are hateful to God; and not only they that do them, but also those that take pleasure in them that do them. . . .

This is the way, beloved, in which we find our Saviour, even Jesus Christ, the High Priest of all our offerings, the defender and helper of our infirmity. By Him we look up to the heights of heaven. By Him we behold, as in a glass, His immaculate and most excellent visage. By Him are the eyes of our hearts opened. By Him our foolish and darkened understanding blossoms up anew towards His marvellous light. By Him the Lord has willed that we should taste of immortal knowledge, "who, being the brightness of His majesty, is by so much greater than the angels, as He hath by inheritance obtained a more excellent name than they."

CLEMENT (*CIRCA* 30–100) is thought by some to be the coworker referred to by Paul in Philippians 4:3. Others believe him to be Clement of Rome, considered by Catholics to be an early successor of Peter as head of the Roman Church. What seems clear is that Clement's *Epistle* was written following a period of persecution, most likely that under Emperor Domitian near the end of the first century. This epistle was widely circulated and read in the early church and was held to be almost on a level with the writings included in the New Testament.

Jesus and the Afterlife

R. C. SPROUL—1988

JESUS PROMISES His disciples that they will one day follow Him to the Father's house in heaven. He declares that, "I go to prepare a place for you." Jesus explains that His departure from their midst, which was troubling their hearts, should be an occasion of great joy. Jesus left them to go to prepare their rooms in heaven.

Jesus not only makes it possible for us to go to heaven, he has actually gone there to assure our reservations and prepare our rooms for us.

I spend about nine months of the year away from my home. Doing so much traveling has a long-range impact on me. I've noticed several patterns emerging in my own psyche about traveling. For one thing, I'm more fussy about advance reservations.

On our trip to heaven we have the best of all possible advance accommodations, prepared by the best of all possible men. Jesus Himself has gone before us to prepare a place in our Father's house.

There are few things more frustrating for a weary traveler than to arrive at a hotel and discover that the hotel has failed to record your reservation or has given your room to somebody else. These mix-ups do occur and are maddening when they happen. But it cannot possibly happen in heaven. If we belong to Christ then we have a rock solid reservation. There are many rooms in the Father's house. There is a place for us that no one else can take away.

For biographical information on this author, see page 12.

Heaven

STEVEN J. LAWSON—1995

MAKE NO MISTAKE ABOUT IT, Heaven is a *real* place. It is not a state of mind. Not a figment of man's imagination. Not a philosophical concept. Not a religious abstraction. Not a sentimental dream. Not the medieval fancy of an ancient scientist. Not the worn-out superstition of a liberal theologian. It's an actual place. A location far more real than where you presently live. . . . It is a *real* place where God lives. It is the *real* place from which Christ came into this world. And it is the *real* place to which Christ returned at His ascension—*really*.

For biographical information on this author, see page 120.

The Purpose of Trials

ERWIN W. LUTZER—1998

THE PURPOSE OF OUR TRIALS and temptations is to train us for ruling with Christ. We are learning the laws of the kingdom, responding in faithful obedience. We are given the opportunity of becoming overcomers so that we might inherit the promises. "For momentary, light affliction is producing for us an eternal weight of glory far beyond all comparison" (2 Corinthians 4:17 NASB). Place all of your trials on one end of the scale and the eternal weight of glory on the other, and it will go "plunk"! It is the weight of a feather versus a cubic foot of gold!

For biographical information on this author, see page 136.

Chapter 12

A Smart Strategy for Treasuring

DALLAS WILLARD—1998

THE FIRST THING that Jesus tells us with respect to treasures is that to treasure things that are "upon the earth" is not a smart strategy for treasuring. Treasures of the earth, by their very nature, simply cannot be held intact. Here is "where moth and rust destroy and where thieves break in and steal" (Matthew 6:19).

We will devote ourselves to the good of . . .
those around us within the range of our power to affect.
These are among God's treasures.

So the wisdom of Jesus is that we should "lay up for ourselves treasures in heaven" (6:20), where forces of nature and human evil cannot harm what we treasure. That is to say, direct your actions toward making a difference in the realm of spiritual substance sustained and governed by God. Invest your life in what God is doing, which cannot be lost.

Of course this means that we will invest in our relationship to Jesus himself, and through him to God. But beyond that, and in close union with it, we will devote ourselves to the good of other people—those around us within the range of our power to affect. These are among God's treasures. . . .

And we also care for this astonishingly rich and beautiful physical realm, the earth itself, of which both we and our neighbors are parts. . . .

This is . . . part of what the apostle Paul calls "sowing to the spirit." And when we do such sowing, "of the spirit we reap what is everlasting." . . . This is, precisely, *how* we deposit treasures in heaven on a daily, hourly basis.

DALLAS WILLARD is professor of philosophy at the University of Southern California. His writings, including *The Spirit of the Disciplines,* have encouraged the recovery of the spiritual disciplines in our time.

Eternal Investments

PAULA RINEHART—1986

MONEY DOES HAVE SPIRITUAL VALUE. In certain ways, money can be invested toward eternal, lasting wealth. For there are many real physical needs that exist in the spiritual Kingdom of God. "Lay up for yourselves treasures in heaven, where neither moth nor rust destroys, and where thieves do not break in and steal" (Matthew 6:20 NKJV). Rather than becoming a servant to money, we can *use* it redemptively for eternal investments in people, in furthering the Kingdom. . . .

We must have eyes to see. The money we exchange for the pizza served to our neighbors builds relationships with *people,* opening a door for the gospel to come to them. Or consider the example of our friend John. He invested money in an airplane ticket to visit a friend who had strayed from God. . . .

So money can be a medium of exchange or a means of investing in matters of lasting, eternal value. When we place money in an offering plate or write a check to a missionary board or take a non-Christian neighbor's children to the zoo, do we see all that is really taking place? God uses the act of giving, of exchanging money, for eternal things—to further His Kingdom not only in the world but in *us* as well.

PAULA RINEHART has touched lives through writing, speaking, and ministering. She is the author of four books and presently has a small Christian counseling practice in North Carolina. Both she and her husband, Stacy, served on staff with the Navigators ministry for over twenty-five years.

Chapter 12

The Truly Rich

Jill Briscoe — 1991

To know Christ is to be rich beyond measure, wealthy beyond your wildest dreams. After all, Jesus is the Jewel of Heaven! Let me tell you a story.

He was the Richest Man in the Valley. There was no disputing it. Secure and confident, he was escorting his house guests to their expensive cars, when John, his gardener, cap in hand, approached him to give him a message. The man was poor and shabbily dressed and looked embarrassed to be talking to the Richest Man in the Valley. He shuffled from one foot to the other.

"Well, out with it, man," his employer snapped impatiently, his eyes on his departing guests.

"Sir," John stuttered. He was obviously *very* nervous.

"Sir—I know this sounds mighty strange, but I had a dream last night that really upset me. I dreamt that the Richest Man in the Valley would die tonight at midnight! You all right, sir?" he finished lamely, feeling exceptionally stupid.

His boss stared at him. John was all right as gardeners go. He worked hard and was honest and trustworthy, but the Richest Man in the Valley was aware that he attended the little evangelical church in the village and was one of those "born-again Christians." He'd never had much time for religion himself, always felt too much church made you a little weird. John's words confirmed his suspicions! "You don't need to worry about me, John," the Richest Man in the Valley said impatiently and cheerfully, turning on his heel.

John watched him disappear inside the huge carved door of the mansion and felt relieved. It had taken all of his courage to talk to the man, but the dream had been so sharp—he'd never experienced anything like it. Had God sent him a message in his dream, he wondered? He worried about the Richest Man in the Valley. He had no idea where he stood with God.

The Richest Man in the Valley closed the door of his beautiful home and looked around. Silly to let the poor man's words bother him.

Why, things had never been better. It wouldn't do any harm, though, he mused, to invite his doctor round for a drink—late in the evening!

So, late that night the Richest Man in the Valley and his doctor enjoyed a game of cards and talked at length about world affairs and the stock market. The clock on the expensive wooden paneling ticked on: five minutes to midnight, four minutes to midnight, three minutes, two minutes. One minute—MIDNIGHT! Irritated with himself that he felt so relieved, the Richest Man in the Valley bade the doctor goodnight and retired. He had no sooner climbed into bed than the doorbell rang urgently. Hurriedly wrapping his robe around him, the Richest Man in the Valley ran downstairs to answer the frantic knocking.

A young girl stood on the doorstep, her eyes red with weeping. Her clothes were old, and she carried what looked like her mother's purse.

"What's the matter?" the Richest Man in the Valley inquired, not unkindly.

"Sir," she gulped, "I just came to tell you that tonight at midnight my father died."

"Your father? Who is your father?" asked the puzzled man.

"John," the little girl replied softly, tears coursing down her face. "John, your gardener—the RICHEST MAN IN THE VALLEY!"

Jill Briscoe has an active speaking and writing ministry that has taken her to many countries. She has written more than forty books, including study guides, devotional material, poetry, and children's books. Along with her husband, Stuart, she serves as minister-at-large for Elmbrook Church in Brookfield, Wisconsin.

Our Works Live On

Dwight L. Moody—1880

We get tired of toiling. Yet there is no real rest on earth. We find in the 4th chapter of Hebrews, beginning with the 9th verse:

"There remaineth therefore a rest to the people of God. For he that is entered into his rest, he also hath ceased from his own works, as God did from his. Let us labor therefore to enter into that rest, lest any man fall after the same example of unbelief."

Now, while we all want rest, I think a great many people make a mistake when they think the church is a place of rest; and when they unite with the church they have a false idea about their position in it. There are a great many that come in to rest. It says here: There remaineth a rest for the people of God, but it don't tell us that the church is a place of rest; we have all eternity to rest in. We are to rest by and by; but we are to work here, and when our work is finished, the Lord will call us home to enjoy that rest. There is no use in talking about rest down here in the enemy's country. We cannot rest in this world, where God's Son has been crucified and cast out. I think that a great many people are going to lose their reward just because they have come into the church with the idea that they are to rest there, as if the church was working for the reward, instead of each one building over against his own house, each one using all his influence toward the building up of Christ's kingdom.

In the 14th chapter of Revelation and the 13th verse, it says:

"And I heard a voice from heaven saying unto me, Write, Blessed are the dead which die in the Lord from henceforth: Yea, saith the Spirit, that they may rest from their labours; and their works do follow them."

Now, death may rob us of money. Death may rob us of position. Death may rob us of our friends; but there is one thing death can never do, and that is, rob us of the work that we do for God. That will live on forever. "Their works will follow them." How much are we doing? Anything that we do outside of ourselves, and not with a mean and selfish motive, *that* is going to live. We have the privilege of setting in motion streams of activity that will flow on when we are dead and gone.

It is the privilege of every one to live more in the future than they do in the present, so that their lives will tell in fifty or a hundred years more than they do now. . . .

If a man lives a mean, selfish life, he goes down to the grave, and his name and everything goes down in the grave with him. If he is ambitious to leave a record behind him, with a selfish motive, his name rots with his body. But if a man just gets outside of himself and begins to work for God, his name will live forever. . . . "Blessed are the dead who die in the Lord. They rest from their labors and their works do follow them." Blessed rest in store; we will rest by and by; but we don't want to talk about rest down here.

We are not going to have the privilege of being co-workers with God in the future—but that is our privilege to-day.

If I am to wipe a tear from the cheek of that fatherless boy, I must do it down here. It is not said in Scripture that we will have the privilege of doing that hereafter. If I am going to help up some fallen man that has been overtaken by sin, I must do it here. We are not taught anywhere in Scripture that we are going to have the glorious privilege of working for God in the world to come. We are not going to have the privilege of being co-workers with God in the future—but that is our privilege to-day. We may not have it to-morrow. It may be taken from us to-morrow; but we can enter into the vineyard and do something to-day before the sun goes down. We can do something now before we go to glory.

DWIGHT L. MOODY (1837–1899) was born in Northfield, Massachusetts, and moved to Chicago in 1855. He became a preacher and began to travel as an evangelist. Together with musician Ira D. Sankey, he made a series of revival tours across the United States, as well as to Great Britain and other countries. Though Moody was not a highly educated man, his direct preaching from Scripture brought people of all social classes to a conversion to Christ. Out of his work grew the Northfield Schools in Massachusetts, and Moody Church and Moody Bible Institute in Chicago.

Chapter 12

A Heavenly Life Now

Wilbur M. Smith—1968

While it is true that hope in itself exercises a tremendous power in the lives of those who have assurance of the hope of good things to come, the Scriptures clearly tell us that the concept of Heaven is for the Christian more than a mere hope. There is a tremendous possibility of heavenly life now. If life in heaven is one of holiness, worship, service, and an overwhelming love for our Redeemer, life here on earth should be, as it were, a preparation for such an eternal environment—a true vestibule leading from this life to the life to come. . . .

One cannot truly believe that at death he will at once enter into heaven and the presence of the Lord without determining deep in his soul that he will make this life, by the grace of God, to be, as it were, a vestibule of heaven to come, even now partaking of the holiness of that eternal state.

Wilbur M. Smith served on the faculties of Moody Bible Institute and Fuller Theological Seminary. He was also professor emeritus of English Bible at Trinity Evangelical Divinity School. He was a well-known author and speaker.

Living in Love and Hope

Lyman Abbott—1903

He was not a philosopher groping after truth, discovering it by research and leaving us to follow his method to the same result; he was a faithful and true witness. "We speak that we do know, and testify that we have seen": this note of personal assurance runs through all his teaching. One has but to compare the consolatory words with which Socrates closes the "Phaedo," and the words with which Christ consoles his disciples in the last interview before his crucifixion, to see the difference between a philosopher searching for the truth concerning an unknown world, and the Divine Man testifying to the truth within his own knowledge respecting that unknown world. I believe that he knew what he was talking about, that he was not deceived by his own illusions, that he was not mistaking his hopes for assurances, that he was not an enthusiast who thought that the phantasmagoria of a day-dream was an assured reality, that when he said, "In my Father's house there are many dwelling-places," he uttered neither the guess of a sibyl, the hope of a prophet, nor the conclusion of a philosopher; he uttered the testimony of a witness to a life of which he had personal and familiar knowledge. . . .

What Scripture and philosophy alike promise to us is eternal life, not eternal sleep, and faith, hope, and love are the essentials of life.

I think of the dead as possessing a more splendid equipment for a larger life of diviner service than was possible to them on earth—a life in which I shall in due time join them if I am counted worthy of their fellowship in the life eternal.

Do they know us, love us, hope for our coming? Shall we know them, love them, and may we hope for their fellowship? Surely. What is there left to be immortal in us if love and hope die? To exist without love and hope is not to live; to exist with hope always disappointed and love always denied would hardly be to live. What Scripture and philosophy alike promise to us is eternal life, not eternal sleep, and faith, hope, and love are the essentials of life.

I would not lay too much stress on the intimations of Scripture. I recognize the difference between its clear revelation and its poetic suggestions; but so far as its suggestions may be counted of value, they all indicate the continuance there of love, which alone makes life worth living here.

Lyman Abbott (1835–1922) gave up the practice of law to be ordained a Congregational minister. He succeeded Henry Ward Beecher as pastor of Plymouth Church, Brooklyn, New York, but in 1899 became editor of *Outlook,* a popular Christian magazine. He understood the Christian faith in its broader implications for social and civil problems.

Mastering Our Fear of Death

WILLIAM GURNALL—1662

LET THY HOPE OF HEAVEN *master thy fear of death.* Why shouldst thou be afraid to die, who hopest to live by dying? Is the apprentice afraid of the day when his time comes out?—he that runs a race, of coming too soon to his goal?—the pilot troubled when he sees his harbour?—or the betrothed virgin grieved when the wedding-day approacheth? Death is all this to thee. When that comes, thy indenture expires, and thy jubilee is come. Thy race is run, and the crown won—sure to drop on thy head when thy soul goes out of thy body. Thy voyage, how troublesome soever it was in the sailing, is now happily finished, and death doth but this friendly office for thee, to uncover and open the ark of thy body, that it may safely land thy soul on the shore of eternity at thy heavenly Father's door—yea, in his sweet embraces, never to be put to sea more. In a word, thy husband is come for thee, and knocks with death's hand at thy door, to come forth unto him, that he may perform his promise, which, in the day of thy betrothing, he made to thee; and thou lovest him but little, if thou beest not willing to be at the trouble of a remove hence, for to enjoy his blissful presence, in his Father's royal palace of heaven, where such preparation is made for thy entertainment, that thou canst not know here, though an angel were sent on purpose to inform thee.

WILLIAM GURNALL (1617–1679) lived during a time of religious conflict in England, leading to revolt against the king and the established Church. Pastor of the parish church at Lavenham in Suffolk, Gurnall was more concerned with his people's souls than with the political conflict. When the Act of Uniformity of 1662 required all ministers to use the current *Book of Common Prayer,* some two thousand Puritan pastors who objected were forced to leave their pulpits. Gurnall remained and as a result lost the respect of subsequent non-Anglican writers. But *The Christian in Complete Armour,* his massive exposition of Ephesians 6:10–20, remains a monument of Puritan writing.

Because He Lives

William J. and Gloria Gaither—*1971*

God sent His Son, they called Him Jesus,
He came to love, heal, and forgive;
He lived and died to buy my pardon,
An empty grave is there to prove my Savior lives.

Because He lives I can face tomorrow,
Because He lives all fear is gone;
Because I know He holds the future,
And life is worth the living just because He lives.

How sweet to hold a newborn baby
And feel the pride and joy he gives;
But greater still the calm assurance;
This child can face uncertain days because He lives.

And then one day I'll cross the river,
I'll fight life's final war with pain;
And then as death gives way to victory,
I'll see the lights of glory and I'll know He lives.

For biographical information on these authors, see pages 189 and 73.

Compiler Biographies

RICHARD C. LEONARD received his Ph.D. in biblical studies from Boston University in 1972. An ordained minister, he served in pastorates in New England and Illinois, and has held teaching appointments at the college and graduate level. He was Scripture editor for *The Complete Library of Christian Worship,* contributing some original entries, and a reviewing editor for the *Praise and Worship Study Bible.* Additionally, he has authored articles in several Christian publications. Now semiretired, Dr. Leonard works as a freelance writer and heads Laudemont Ministries (www.laudemont.org), an organization devoted to worship studies and biblical theology. He and his wife, Shirley Anne, make their home in Wheaton, Illinois.

JONANCY LINN SUNDBERG received her degree from Wheaton College (Illinois). She pursued a career as an educator, frequently lecturing at teacher-training courses in churches. Her work in churches has also included numerous volunteer leadership and administrative positions. She has extensive experience in Christian communications as well as in radio, community-theater stage productions, and reader's theater. Currently, she is in demand as a speaker for various inspirational and entertainment events. She is credited with producing three other compilations: *Suddenly a Widow, Hope in Times of Grief,* and *Encouragement for Pastors.* She resides in Arkansas with her feline family.

Sources

Chapter 1: The Call of Heaven

Athenagoras. "Confutation of the Other Charges Brought Against the Christians," in *Plea on Behalf of Christians,* from *Ante-Nicene Fathers: The Writings of the Fathers down to A.D. 325,* Chapter 31. Translated by B. P. Pratten. Edited by Alexander Roberts and James Donaldson. Revised and Chronologically Arranged, with Brief Prefaces and Occasional Notes by A. Cleveland Coxe. Peabody, MA: Hendrickson, 1999. Reprint of the American Edition, Vol. 2, *Fathers of the Second Century: Hermas, Tatian, Athenagoras, Theophilus, and Clement of Alexandria (Entire).* Chronologically Arranged, with Notes, Prefaces and Elucidations, by A. Cleveland Coxe. Originally published by Christian Literature, 1885.

Baillie, John. Cited in Lil Copan and Anna Trimiew, comps. *Images of Heaven: Reflections on Glory,* 69. Colorado Springs: Harold Shaw, a division of WaterBrook, 1996.

Bayly, Joseph. *Heaven.* Colorado Springs: Cook Communications Ministries, 1977. Used with permission. May not be further reproduced. All rights reserved.

Cleghorn, John Hyde. 1995. Used by permission.

Cyprian, Treatise VII. *On the Mortality,* in *Ante-Nicene Fathers: The Writings of the Fathers down to A.D. 325,* Chapters 24–26, 475. Translated by Ernest Wallis. Edited by Alexander Roberts and James Donaldson. Revised and Chronologically Arranged, with Brief Prefaces and Occasional Notes by A. Cleveland Coxe. Peabody, MA: Hendrickson, 1999. Reprint of the American Edition, Vol. 5, *Fathers of the Third Century: Hippolytus, Cyprian, Caius, Novatian, Appendix.* Chronologically Arranged, with Brief Notes and Prefaces, by A. Cleveland Coxe. Originally published by Christian Literature, 1886.

Dickinson, Emily. "This World Is Not Conclusion," No. 501 in *The Complete Poems of Emily Dickinson.* Edited by Thomas H. Johnson, 243. Boston: Little, Brown, 1960.

Lewis, C. S. *The Problem of Pain,* 144–48. New York: Macmillan, 1962.

Packer J. I. *I Want to Be a Christian,* 101–102 (Wheaton, IL: Tyndale, 1977).

Piper, Don. *90 Minutes in Heaven.* With Cecil Murphey. Grand Rapids: Fleming Revell, a division of Baker, 2004.

Rossetti, Christina Georgina. "Heaven Overarches," in *The Poetical Works,* 286. New York: Alder's Foreign Books, 1970.

Shipton, Anna. "Spirit Voices," in *Whispers in the Palms,* 5th ed., 79–80. London: Morgan and Scott [c. 1875], (2d ed. appeared in 1857; date of first edition unknown).

Sproul, R. C. *Surprised by Suffering,* 135–38. Wheaton, IL: Tyndale, 1988.

Tada, Joni Eareckson. Quoted in Bill Gaither et al., *Heaven,* 72. Nashville: J. Countryman, a division of Thomas Nelson Publishers, Inc., 2003. Reprinted by permission. All rights reserved.

Tennyson, Alfred. "In Memoriam," in *The Poetical Works of Alfred Tennyson, Poet Laureate,* 105. New York: Harper & Brothers, 1872.

Chapter 2: The Glory of Heaven

Bunyan, John. "Of Heaven." In *One Thing Is Needful; or, Serious Meditations Upon the Four Lasting Things: Death, Judgment, Heaven, and Hell,* in *The Complete Works of John Bunyan,* 991. Philadelphia: Bradley, Garretson, 1876. (Originally published London: Nath, Ponder, at the Peacock in the Poultry, 1688).

Cowper, William. "Hear What God the Lord Hath Spoken," [based on Isaiah 60:15–20] in *Olney Hymns.* London: J. Johnson, 1806. (Originally published London: W. Oliver, 1779).

Damiani, Peter. *The Song of S. Peter Damiani on the Joy and Glory of Paradise (De Gaudio Paridisi).* Translated by Thomas Rogers, in *A Right Christian Treatise, entituled S. Augustines Praiers.* London: 1581. Reproduced in Stephen A. Hurlbut, ed., *The Picture of the Heavenly Jerusalem in the Writings of Johannes of Fecamp, De Contemplativa Vita and in the Elizabethan Hymns.* Washington, D.C.: St. Albans, 1943.

Edwards, Jonathan. "True Saints, When Absent from the Body, Are Present with the Lord" (Sermon 6). Printed source not available. Copied from the Christian Classics Ethereal Library at Calvin College, Select

Sermons of Jonathan Edwards. http://www.ccel.org/e/edwards/absent_body/absent_body1.0.pdf.

Evans, Tony. *The Best Is Yet to Come,* 248–49. Chicago: Moody, 2000.

Excerpted from *Dominion* © 1996 by Randy Alcorn. Used by permission of WaterBrook Multnomah Publishing Group, a division of Random House Inc. Randy Alcorn is the bestselling author of *Heaven* and the novels *Deadline, Dominion,* and *Deception.* www.epm.org.

MacArthur, John F. *The Glory of Heaven,* 111, 143–44, 68. Wheaton, IL: Crossway Books, a division of Good News Publishers, 1996. Used by permission. www.crossway.com.

MacDonald, George. *Unspoken Sermons (Series 3).* London: Longmans, Green, 1891.

Prior, Matthew. "Charity, a Paraphrase on the Thirteenth Chapter of the First Epistle to the Corinthians." In *Heaven in Song: Comprising the Gems of All Ages on the Better Land,* compiled by Henry C. Fish, 106. New York: Belford, Clarke, 1888.

Tada, Joni Eareckson, and Steven D. Estes. *When God Weeps.* Copyright © 1997 by Joni Eareckson Tada and Steve Estes. Used by permission of Zondervan.

Chapter 3: Longing for Heaven

Baillie, John. *And the Life Everlasting,* 340–42. New York: Charles Scribner's Sons, 1933. Reprint, 1951.

Beam, Joe. *Seeing the Unseen.* New York: Howard Books, a division of Simon & Schuster Inc., 2000. Reprinted with permission.

Dickinson, Emily. "Going to Heaven," No. 79 in *The Complete Poems of Emily Dickinson,* 41. Edited by Thomas H. Johnson. Boston: Little, Brown, 1960.

Haney, David. *A Living Hope,* 32, 33, 140, 141, 144, 145. Wheaton, IL: Crossway Books, a division of Good News Publishers, 1999. Used by permission. www.crossway.com.

Leonard, Shirley Anne. "Golden Streets." In "Poetry by Shirley Anne Leonard." Copyright © 2002 Laudemont Ministries, www.laudemont.org.

Meyfart, Johann Matthäus. "Jerusalem, Whose Towers Touch the Skies" [*Jerusalem, du hochgebaute Stadt*]. Translated by Gilbert E. Doan. *Lutheran Book of Worship,* No. 348. Minneapolis: Augsburg; Philadelphia, Board of Publication of the Lutheran Church in America, 1978. [An older translation exists known as "Jerusalem, Thou City Fair and High"]. Used by permission.

Miller, Calvin. Section introduction in Lil Copan and Anna Trimiew, comps. *Images of Heaven: Reflections on Glory,* 102–104, 106. Colorado Springs: Harold Shaw, a division of WaterBrook, 1996.

Muhlenberg, William Augustus. "I Would Not Live Alway." In *An American Anthology, 1787–1900,* edited by Edmund Clarence Stedman, 74. New York: Houghton Mifflin, 1900.

Proctor, Edna Dean. "Heaven, O Lord, I Cannot Lose." In *An American Anthology, 1787–1900,* edited by Edmund Clarence Stedman. New York: Houghton Mifflin, 1900.

Ten Boom, Corrie. *The Hiding Place.* With John and Elizabeth Sherrill. 215–17. Minneapolis: World Wide Publications, 1971.

Tennyson, Alfred. *The Poetical Works of Alfred Tennyson,* 814. Boston: Houghton Mifflin, n.d. Originally published in *Demeter and Other Poems* (London: Macmillan, 1889).

Vaughan, Henry. *Sacred Poems,* 152–54 London: G. Bell and Sons, 1914. [Poem is untitled; called "Departed Friends" by the editors.]

Chapter 4: At Home in Heaven

"A Pilgrim Here I Wander," in *Lyra Germanica.* Translated by Catherine Winkworth. From *Heaven in Song: Comprising the Gems of All Ages on the Better Land,* 471–73. Compiled by Henry C. Fish. Chicago, New York, San Francisco: Belford, Clarke, 1888.

Bounds, Edward McKendree. *Heaven—A Place, a City, a Home,* Chapters 10 and 14, 44–45, 52, 53. Grand Rapids: Baker, 1975 (Originally published New York, 1921).

Crosby, Fanny J. "Blessed Homeland," No. 25 in *Welcome Tidings: A New Collection of Sacred Songs for the Sunday School.* Edited by Robert Lowry, W. Howard Doane, and Ira D. Sankey. New York: Biglow & Main; Cincinnati: John Church & Co., 1877.

Excerpted from *Dominion* © 1996 by Randy Alcorn. Used by permission of WaterBrook Multnomah Publishing Group, a division of Random House Inc. Randy Alcorn is the bestselling author of *Heaven* and the novels *Deadline, Dominion,* and *Deception.* www.epm.org.

Faber, Frederick W. "The Shore of Eternity"? in *The Home Beyond, or Views of Heaven and Its Relation to Earth,* 275. Compiled by Samuel Fallows. Chicago: M. A. Donohue, 1889.

Gaither, Gloria, and Buddy Greene. *I Don't Belong (Sojourner's Song).* Copyright © 1990 by Gaither Music, Rufus Music, SpiritQuest Music.

Adm. by Gaither Copyright Management. In Bill Gaither et al., *Heaven,* 31. Nashville: J. Countryman, 2003.

Hewitt, Eliza E. "When We All Get to Heaven," No. 546 in *Hymns for the Living Church.* Edited by Donald P. Hustad. Carol Stream, IL: Hope, 1974. Originally published in William Kirkpatrick and Henry Gilmour, eds., *Pentecostal Praises.* Philadelphia: Hall-Mack, 1898. Found in many hymnals (public domain). Also in The Cyber Hymnal, http://www.cyberhymnal.org/htm/w/w/wwag2hvn.htm.

Kreeft, Peter. *Heaven: The Heart's Deepest Longing,* 66–67. San Francisco: Ignatius, 1989. Used with permission.

Lewis, C. S. *The Last Battle,* 161–62, 173. New York: Macmillan, 1956.

Rossetti, Christina Georgina. "Up-Hill," in *The Poetical Works,* 339. New York: Alder's Foreign Books, 1970.

Stowell, Joseph M. *Eternity: Reclaiming a Passion for What Endures,* 88, 91–92. Grand Rapids: Discovery House, 1995, 2006. Used by permission of Discovery House Publishers, Grand Rapids, MI, 49501.

Vanauken, Sheldon. *A Severe Mercy,* 202–203. San Francisco: HarperSanFrancisco, 1977.

Chapter 5: Our Glory in Heaven

George, Timothy. "Good Question." *Christianity Today,* February 2003, 84.

Johnson, L. D., *The Morning After Death,* 145–47. Macon, GA: Smyth & Helwys, 1978, 1990.

Luther, Martin. "Enemies of the Cross of Christ" (Sermon for the 23rd Sunday after Trinity), sections 31–35 in *Sermons of Martin Luther.* Edited by John Nicholas Lenker. Taken from *Sermons on Epistle Texts,* Vol. 8, 356–57. Reprinted in Grand Rapids: Baker, 1983. Reproduction of *Luther's Epistle Sermons,* Vol. 3. Minneapolis: The Luther Press, 1909.

Origen. *The Fundamental Doctrines,* Chapter 6, "On the End of the World," sections 5–6 in *Ante-Nicene Fathers: The Writings of the Fathers down to A.D. 325.,* 346–47. Edited by Alexander Roberts and James Donaldson. Revised and Chronologically Arranged, with Brief Prefaces and Occasional Notes by A. Cleveland Coxe. Peabody, MA: Hendrickson, 1999. Reprint of the American Edition, Vol. 4, *Fathers of the Third Century: Tertullian, Part Fourth; Minucius Felix; Commodian; Orgen, Parts First and Second, American Edition.* Chronologically Arranged, with Brief Notes and Prefaces, by A. Cleveland Coxe. (Originally published by Christian Literature, 1885.)

Sanders, J. Oswald. *Heaven: Better By Far,* 88–89, 92. Grand Rapids: Discovery House, 1993. Used by permission. All rights reserved.

Sproul, R. C. *Surprised by Suffering,* 141–43. Wheaton, IL: Tyndale, 1988.

Spurgeon, Charles Haddon. "Paul's Desire to Depart," Sermon #274. Delivered on Sabbath Morning, September 11, 1859 at the Music Hall, Royal Surrey Gardens. *Spurgeon's Sermons,* Vol. 5:1859. Grand Rapids: Christian Classics Ethereal Library, Calvin College, http://www.ccel.org/ccel/spurgeon/sermons05.xlix.html.

Wesley, John. "On the Resurrection of the Dead," [adapted in 1732 from Benjamin Calamy, 1704], Sermon 134 in *Sermons on Several Occasions.* New York: Carleton & Porter, n.d. [Text copied from http://www.ccel.org/w/wesley/sermons/sermons-html/serm-137.html.]

Chapter 6: Loved Ones in Heaven

Anspach, F. R. *The Sepulchres of Our Departed,* 3d ed., 306–11. Philadelphia: Lindsay & Blakiston, 1854. The quotation from Wordsworth consists of excerpts from "We Are Seven," from *Lyrical Ballads* (London, 1798), a work published jointly with Samuel Taylor Coleridge.

Beecher, Henry Ward. Undocumented quotation in *The Home Beyond, or Views of Heaven and its Relation to Earth,* 395. Compiled by Samuel Fallows. Chicago: M. A. Donohue, 1889.

Browns, Ralph Emerson. "The Early Bereft," in *Joy with Words,* 15. Bloomington, IL: Illinois Wesleyan University Press, 1965.

Evans, Tony. *Tony Evans Speaks Out on Heaven and Hell,* 35–36. Chicago: Moody, 2000.

Fraser, Valerie. "Southern Journal." *Southern Living,* October 2000, 208.

Knight, Walter B. Excerpt taken from *Great Preaching on Heaven.* Compiled by Curtis Hutson. Murfreesboro, TN: Sword of the Lord, 1987.

"Lambs of the Upper Fold," in *Heaven in Song: Comprising the Gems of All Ages on the Better Land,* 278–79. Compiled by Henry C. Fish. Chicago, New York, San Francisco: Belford, Clarke, 1888.

MacDonald, George. "A Voice," in *Sir Gibbie,* Chapter 27, 188–92. New York: A. L. Burt, n.d. (First published in London: Hurst and Blackett, 1880). http://www.ccel.org/ccel/macdonald/sirgibbie.xxviii.html [NOTE: Bethany House republished *Sir Gibbie* under the title *The Baronet's Song,* abridging the book and modernizing the language from the hard-to-read Scottish dialect. This passage was not included in the abridgement, so Dr. Richard Leonard created the above updated version.]

Paterson-Smyth, J. *The Gospel of the Hereafter,* 98–99, 105, 220–21. New York: Fleming H. Revell, 1910.

Piggott, William C. "For Those We Love Within the Veil," No. 222 in *The Hymnal of the Protestant Episcopal Church, 1940.* New York: Church Pension Fund, 1961. Also in The Cyber Hymnal (public domain), http://www.cyberhymnal.org/htm/f/o/forthose.htm.

Strobel, Lee P. *The Case for Christ*. Copyright © 1998 by Lee Strobel. Used by permission of Zondervan.

Wesley, Charles. "Come, Let Us Join Our Friends Above." First published in *Funeral Hymns,* 1759. This version in John Wesley, ed., *A Collection of Hymns, for the Use of the People Called Methodists.* Originally published in 1780. Copied from 1889 edition. Issued in London: Wesleyan-Methodist Book-Room. Reproduced on Christian Classics Ethereal Library at Calvin College, http://www.ccel.org/w/wesley/hymn/jwg09/jwg0947.html.

Chapter 7: Hosts of Heaven

Alighieri, Dante. *Paradiso* from *The Divine Comedy,* Canto 31, 593. Translated by Henry Wadsworth Longfellow. Boston and New York: Houghton Mifflin, 1893.

Bunyan, John. *The Pilgrim's Progress,* Part I, The Tenth Stage, 161, 164–67. Philadelphia, Chicago: John C. Winston, 1933.

Gilmore, John. *Probing Heaven: Key Questions on the Hereafter,* 128–30. Grand Rapids: Baker, 1989.

Gire, Ken. *Life as We Would Want It.* Nashville: Thomas Nelson Inc., 2006. All rights reserved. Reprinted by permission.

Jenkins, Margie Little. *You Only Die Once.* Nashville: Integrity, a division of Thomas Nelson Inc., 2002. All rights reserved. Reprinted by permission.

Lawson, Steven J. *Heaven Help Us!* 52–57. Colorado Springs: NavPress, 1995.

Libby, Larry and Wayne Mcloughlin. *Someday Heaven*. Copyright © 2001 by Larry Libby. Used by permission of Zondervan.

Milton, John. *Paradise Regained,* Book 1, in *The Poetical Works of John Milton,* 296–97. Boston: D. Lothrop, 1883.

Spenser, Edmund. *An Hymn of Heavenly Love,* from *Four Hymns.* In *The Poetical Works of Edmund Spenser,* 304–306. Edited by George Gilfillan. London: James Nisbet, 1859. Originally published as *An Hymne of Heavenly Love,* from *Fowre Hymnes* (London, Printed for William Ponsonby, 1596).

Tada, Joni Eareckson. *Heaven . . . Your Real Home*. Copyright © 2001. Used by permission of Zondervan.

Chapter 8: Treasure in Heaven

Alcorn, Randy. *Edge of Eternity,* 293–97. Colorado Springs: WaterBrook, 1998. Randy Alcorn is the bestselling author of *Heaven* and the novels *Deadline, Dominion,* and *Deception.* www.epm.org.

Bernard of Clairvaux. "Of the Attainment of this Perfection of Love Only at the Resurrection." In *On Loving God,* Chapter 11, 50–54. Edited by Hugh Martin. Westport, CT: Greenwood, 1981 [Reprint of SCM Press edition, 1959].

Calvin, John. "Of the Last Resurrection," Chapter 25, 273–74. From *The Mode of Obtaining the Grace of Christ. The Benefits It Confers, and the Effects Resulting from It* in *Institutes of the Christian Religion,* Vol. 2, Book 3. Translated by Henry Beveridge. Grand Rapids: Eerdmans, 1972 [reprint]. Originally printed in London by Arnold Hatfield (for Bonham Norton, 1599).

Crosby, Fanny J. "How Oft We Are There," No. 30 in *Winning Songs.* Edited by John R. Sweney, William J. Kirkpatrick, and H. L. Gilmour. Philadelphia: John J. Hood, 1892.

Cyril of Jerusalem. *The Catechetical Lectures,* Lecture 18. Translated by Edwin Hamilton Gifford. "On the Words, and in One Holy Catholic Church, and in the Resurrection of the Flesh, and the Life Everlasting," Sections 29–31 of the *Nicene and Post-Nicene Fathers,* Second Series. Edited by Philip Schaff and Henry Wace. Peabody, MA: Hendrickson, 1999. Reprint of the American Edition, Vol. 2, *Cyril of Jerusalem, Gregory Nazianzen.* Originally published by Christian Literature [1885].

Lockerbie, Bruce and Lory Lockerbie. *Take Heart.* Grand Rapids: Fleming H. Revell, a division of Baker, 1990.

Lutzer, Erwin W. *Your Eternal Reward,* 13–15. Chicago: Moody Press, 1998.

MacArthur, John F. *The Glory of Heaven,* 102. Wheaton, IL: Crossway Books, 1996. Used by permission. Crossway Books is a division of Good News Publishers, Wheaton, IL 60187. www.crosswaybooks.org.

Ryle, J. C. *Heaven* ("Helmington Series" Tract). Printed source could not be located. Copied from Bible Bulletin Board, http://www.biblebb.com/files/ryle/heaven.htm.

Tada, Joni Eareckson, and Steven D. Estes. *When God Weeps.* Copyright

© 1997 by Joni Eareckson Tada and Steve Estes. Used by permission of Zondervan.

Traherne, Thomas. "The Fifth Century," Sections 2, 6–8 in *Centuries of Meditations.* Edited by Bertram Dobell. London: Published by the Editor, 1908. Printed source not available; this material copied digitally from Christian Classics Ethereal Library, Calvin College, http://www.ccel.org/t/traherne/centuries/centuries.htm.

Chapter 9: The Heavenly City

Alcorn, Randy. *In Light of Eternity: Perspectives on Heaven,* 31–32. Colorado Springs: WaterBrook, 1999. Randy Alcorn is the bestselling author of *Heaven* and the novels *Deadline, Dominion,* and *Deception.* www.epm.org.

Bernard of Cluny. "Jerusalem the Golden" (*Urbs Sion aurea*). Translated by John Mason Neale. [This version consists of selected stanzas from the public domain source The Cyber Hymnal, http://www.cyberhymnal.org, with addition of the final stanza from No. 430 in *The Hymnbook of the Presbyterian Church,* 1955. The order of stanzas is uncertain because the original Latin could not be found, nor the original translation by John Mason Neale.]

Bonar, Horatius. ["The New Jerusalem"]. In *Heaven in Song: Comprising the Gems of All Ages on the Better Land,* 276. Compiled by Henry C. Fish. New York: Belford, Clarke, 1888.

De Haan, Martin. *Been Thinking About.* Copyright © 2007 by RBC Ministries, Grand Rapids, MI. Reprinted by permission. All rights reserved.

Gilmore, John. *Probing Heaven: Key Questions on the Hereafter,* 122, 114–15. Grand Rapids: Baker, 1989.

Hildegard of Bingen. "O Jerusalem." Translation printed in booklet accompanying *A Feather on the Breath of God: Sequences and Hymns by Abbess Hildegard of Bingen* [Compact Disk], Hyperion Records. Original recording issued 1981. The full Latin texts can be found in *Patrologia,* Vol. 197. Edited by Migne. Paris, 1855; *Corpus Christianorum, continuatio mediaevalis.* Published in Turnholt, Belgium. [Passages addressed to St. Rupert, patron of Hildegard's abbey, have been omitted in above.]

Hopkins, John Henry Jr. "Thy Gates of Glistening Pearl Unfold." In *Heaven in Song: Comprising the Gems of All Ages on the Better Land,* 172–74.

Compiled by Henry C. Fish. Chicago, New York, San Francisco: Belford, Clarke, 1888.

Lewis, C. S. *The Problem of Pain,* 134–35. New York: Simon & Schuster, 1996.

MacArthur, John F. *The Glory of Heaven,* 89, 103–104. Wheaton, IL: Crossway Books, a division of Good News Publishers, 1996. Used by permission. www.crossway.com.

Chapter 10: Worship in Heaven

Alcorn, Randy. *Edge of Eternity,* 312–13. Colorado Springs: WaterBrook, 1998. Randy Alcorn is the bestselling author of *Heaven* and the novels *Deadline, Dominion,* and *Deception.* www.epm.org.

Attributed to Franz, Ignaz. "Holy God, We Praise Thy Name" (Grosser Gott, wir loben Dich), a versification of the *Te Deum* in Maria Theresa's *Katholisches Gesangbuch* (Vienna, *circa* 1774). Translated by Clarence A. Walworth, 1858. Found in many hymnals. This version from No. 8 in *The Methodist Hymnal* (Nashville: Methodist Publishing House, 1964).

Augustine. "Of the Eternal Felicity of the City of God, and of the Perpetual Sabbath." In *The City of God,* Book 22, Chapter 30. Translated by Marcus Dods. Taken from the *Nicene and Post-Nicene Fathers,* First Series. Edited by Philip Schaff. Peabody, MA: Hendrickson, 1999. Reprint of the American Edition, Vol. 2, *St. Augustine's City of God and Christian Doctrine.* Originally published by Christian Literature, 1887.

Francis de Sales. "That We Cannot Attain to Perfect Union with God in this Mortal Life." In *Treatise on the Love of God,* Book 3, Chapter 6. Translated by Henry Benedict Mackey. Originally published as the *Library of St. Francis de Sales,* Vol. 2. (London: Burns & Oates, and New York: Benziger Brothers, *circa* 1884).

How, William Walsham. "For All Thy Saints." In *The Sarum Hymnal,* No. 299. Edited by Theodore Edward Aylward. Salisbury [England]: W. P. Aylward; and Brown and Co.; London, Simpkin, Marshall & Co. and Metzer & Co., 1869. [The sixth stanza ("O may Thy soldiers . . . ") does not appear in the above source, but is found in *The Hymnal of the Protestant Episcopal Church,* 1940. New York: Church Pension Fund, 1961.]

Landstad, Magnus B. "Full Many Shall Come" ("Der Mange Skal Komme"). In *Service Book and Hymnal of the Lutheran Church in America,* 1958, No. 333. Translated from Norwegian by Peer Olsen Strömme, 1909, and altered by Lawrence N. Field. The hymnal includes only four stanzas.

The full digital text appears in The Cyber Hymnal, URL http://www.cyberhymnal.org/htm/f/u/fullmany.htm.

Lawson, Steven J. *Heaven Help Us!* 60–61. Colorado Springs: NavPress, 1995.

Lutzer, Erwin W. *Your Eternal Reward,* 46–47, 55–56. Chicago: Moody, 1998.

Miller, Calvin. Section introduction in Lil Copan and Anna Trimiew, comps. *Images of Heaven: Reflections on Glory,* 138–42. Colorado Springs: Harold Shaw, a division of WaterBrook, 1996.

Sproul, R. C. *Surprised by Suffering.* Wheaton, IL: Tyndale, 1988.

Spurgeon, Charles Haddon. "Heavenly Worship," Sermon No. 110. Delivered on Sabbath Morning, December 28th, 1856, at the Music Hall, Royal Surrey Gardens. Grand Rapids: Christian Classics Ethereal Library, Calvin College, http://www.ccel.org/ccel/spurgeon/sermons03.iv.html.

Tada, Joni Eareckson. *Heaven . . . Your Real Home.* Copyright © 2001. Used by permission of Zondervan.

The Celebration Hymnal, No. 314. Word Music/Integrity Music, 1997.

Watts, Isaac. Psalm 145 ["I'll Praise My Maker"] in *The Psalms of David.* Boston: Lincoln & Edmands, 1813 [Original publication in England, 1719].

Chapter 11: Not in Heaven

Beam, Joe. *Seeing the Unseen.* New York: Howard Books, a division of Simon & Schuster Inc., 2000. Reprinted with permission.

Gaither, William J. "It Will Be Worth It All" (copyright by author), No. 135 in *Hymns for the Family of God.* Nashville: Paragon Associates Inc.

Hamline, L. L. "No Regret in Heaven" (extract from a sermon). In *The Home Beyond, or Views of Heaven and its Relation to Earth,* 243–44. Compiled by Samuel Fallows. Chicago: M. A. Donohue, 1889.

Haney, David. *A Living Hope,* 142–43. Wheaton, IL: Crossway Books, a division of Good News Publishers, 1999. Used by permission. www.crossway.com.

Julian of Norwich. *Showings,* Chapter 20, 160–61. Translated by Edmund Colledge and James Walsh. New York, Ramsey, NJ, Toronto: Paulist Press, 1978. Also sometimes called *Revelations of Divine Love* or *Showings of Love.*

Lockyer, Herbert. *Dying, Death, and Destiny,* 114. Grand Rapids: Fleming H. Revell, a division of Baker Publishing Group, 1980.

MacArthur, John F. *The Glory of Heaven,* 115. Wheaton, IL: Crossway Books, a division of Good News Publishers, 1996. Used by permission. www.crossway.com.

Stowe, Harriet Beecher. *The Minister's Wooing.* New York: Derby and

Jackson, 1859. Reproduced in W. Robertson Nicoll, *Reunion in Eternity,* 239 (New York: George H. Doran, 1919).

Teasdale, Sara. "If I Must Go." In *Mirror of the Heart: Poems of Sara Teasdale,* 77. Edited by William Drake. New York: Macmillan; London: Collier Macmillan, 1984.

Chapter 12: Influence of Heaven

Abbott, Lyman. *The Other Room,* 52–53, 92–93. New York: Outlook Company, 1903.

Barnes, M. Craig. *An Extravagant Mercy.* Copyright © 2003 by Gospel Light, Ventura, CA 93003. Used by permission.

Briscoe, Jill. *Heartbeat,* 21–24. Wheaton, IL: Harold Shaw, 1991.

Clement. *The First Epistle of Clement to the Corinthians,* Chapters 35–36, 14–16 in the *Ante-Nicene Fathers: The Writings of the Fathers down to A.D.* 325. Edited by Alexander Roberts and James Donaldson. Revised and Chronologically Arranged, with Brief Prefaces and Occasional Notes by A. Cleveland Coxe. Peabody, MA: Hendrickson, 1999. Reprint of the American Edition, Vol. 1, *The Apostolic Fathers with Justin Martyr and Irenaeus.* Chronologically Arranged, with Brief Notes and Prefaces, by A. Cleveland Coxe. Originally published by Christian Literature, 1886.

Gaither, William J., and Gloria Gaither. "Because He Lives" (copyright, 1971 by William J. Gaither), in Bill Gaither et al., *Heaven,* 83. Nashville: J. Countryman, 2003.

Gurnall, William. *The Christian in Complete Armour: A Treatise of the Saints' War against the Devil,* Direction Ninth, "The Several Pieces of the Whole Armour of God," Fifth Piece, "The Christian's Helmet," 170–71. London: Banner of Truth Trust, 1964. Reprint of edition from Glasgow: Blackie & Sons, 1864. Originally published in three volumes, 1655–1662.

Lawson, Steven J. *Heaven Help Us!* Colorado Springs: NavPress, 1995.

Lutzer, Erwin. *Your Eternal Reward,* 57. Chicago: Moody, 1998.

Moody, D. L. *Heaven: Where It Is, Its Inhabitants, and How to Get There,* 86–87, 88. Chicago: F. H. Revell, 1880.

Rinehart, Paula, and Stacy Rinehart. *Living in Light of Eternity,* 98–100. Colorado Springs: NavPress, 1986.

Smith, Wilbur M. *The Biblical Doctrine of Heaven,* 139, 154. Chicago: Moody, 1968.

Sproul, R. C. *Surprised by Suffering.* Wheaton, IL: Tyndale, 1988.

Willard, Dallas. *The Divine Conspiracy,* 204–205. New York: HarperCollins, 1998.